In *Failosophy*, Eliza[beth Day brings]
together all the less[ons she has learned]
from conversations [on]
her award-winning *How to Fail* podcast,
from stories shared with her by readers and
listeners, and from her own life, and distils
them into seven principles of failure.

Practical, reassuring and inspirational,
these principles offer a guide through
life's rough patches. From failed exams to
romantic break-ups, from career setbacks
to confidence crises, from navigating anxiety
to surviving loss, *Failosophy* recognises,
and celebrates, the fact that failure connects
us all. It is what makes us human.

With insights from **MALCOLM GLADWELL**,
PHOEBE WALLER-BRIDGE, **LEMN SISSAY**,
FRANKIE BRIDGE, **NIGEL SLATER**,
EMELI SANDÉ, **ALAIN DE BOTTON**, **MABEL**,
FEARNE COTTON, **MEERA SYAL**,
DAME KELLY HOLMES, **ANDREW SCOTT** and
many, many more, *Failosophy* is the essential
handbook for turning failure into success.

FAILOSOPHY

ALSO BY ELIZABETH DAY

How to Fail: Everything I've Ever Learned From Things
Going Wrong
Scissors, Paper, Stone
Home Fires
Paradise City
The Party

FAILOSOPHY

A Handbook For When Things Go Wrong

ELIZABETH DAY

4th ESTATE • *London*

4th Estate
An imprint of HarperCollins*Publishers*
1 London Bridge Street
London SE1 9GF

www.4thEstate.co.uk

First published in Great Britain in 2020 by 4th Estate

4

A catalogue record for this book is
available from the British Library

ISBN 978-0-00-842038-3

Set in Adobe Garamond Pro
Printed and bound in Great Britain by
CPI Group (UK) Ltd, Croydon

MIX
Paper from
responsible sources
FSC™ C007454

This book is produced from independently certified FSC™ paper
to ensure responsible forest management.

Find out more about HarperCollins and the environment at
www.harpercollins.co.uk/green

For Justin, who never fails me

Contents

Introduction

Every day since 13 July 2018, I have thought about failure. My own and other people's. The failures that define us and the ones that seem stupid in hindsight. Everything from failed marriages to failed driving tests.

I can name the date so precisely because that is the day on which I launched a podcast called *How To Fail*. In fact, it was called *How To Fail With Elizabeth Day* because with near-perfect comic timing, I had failed to name it properly, having earlier failed to do my research, which would have uncovered another podcast already in existence called almost the same thing.

Blissfully unaware of this fact, I drew my logo with felt-tip pens one night, tracing around the bottom of my favourite mug to draw a rosette badge. I wrote the title in my own handwriting, haphazardly colouring it in with pink highlighter. I sold the wedding dress from my failed marriage on eBay to fund the first few episodes. At first, it failed to attract any bids so I slashed the price and then, when someone bought it, I wrapped it up in a bulky package and took it to the post office feeling a sense of release as I did so. My marriage might have failed, but at least one good thing had come out of it.

Having failed to find an original name, failed to get the desired price for the wedding dress and failed to hire a graphic designer to produce a more professional logo, I was all set for the failure of the podcast itself. I didn't expect *How To Fail With Elizabeth Day*, or the subsequent memoir that came out of it, to be the most successful thing I have ever done, but that's how it turned out.

Never let it be said that the universe doesn't have a sense of irony.

At the time of writing, the podcast has been going for 18 months and is well into its seventh season. It has attracted many millions of downloads despite, or perhaps because of, its relatively simple concept. Each week, I ask my guest to come up with three 'failures' in advance of the recording. These can be sublime or ridiculous; profound or superficial. The only criteria are that the guest must feel comfortable talking about the subjects they've chosen, and that they are able to reflect on what they have learned from them.

The idea is to make listeners who are scared of failure in their own lives feel less alone, and also to reassure them that there might be hope on the other side. It was based on the premise that learning how we fail actually means learning how to succeed better. Most failures can teach us something meaningful about ourselves if we choose to listen and, besides, success tastes all the sweeter if you've fought for it.

The people I've spoken to have told me about their family dysfunction, their mental health issues and the grief they have grappled with after profound loss – a son who died during a routine operation at the age of 21; a baby lost to miscarriage; 10 years lost to the grip of heroin addiction. I, too, have examined my own failures both professional and personal, failures of faith and intimacy, and sometimes just a failure of self-belief that repeated itself on what seemed like an automatic spin cycle until the world shuddered to a halt and I was confronted with who I actually was as opposed to the blameless, pleasant, undemanding projection of the perfect person I'd tried so hard to be.

Alongside this, I have thought about the failure of my marriage; my failure to have children; my failure to realise that a desire to people-please was making me desperately unhappy; my failure to resolve things with an ex-boyfriend who was killed six months after we broke up; my failure to express my own anger, instead masking it with a more socially acceptable sadness; and my failure to remove myself from toxic relationships until it was a question of survival.

All these failures have been an integral part of my life. All these failures have been part of my growth. Life is texture. Experiencing all facets of existence – the good and the bad – enables us to appreciate them fully. I feel lucky in my current relationship not only because I have met a wonderful person, but also because I have so much experience of dysfunctional relationships with not-so-wonderful people to compare it to.

'The darker the night,' Dostoyevsky wrote, 'the brighter the stars.'

Being at peace with failure means I have very few regrets. Each time something has gone wrong, it has led me to where I am meant to be, which is right here, right now, writing this introduction. I firmly cling to the belief that the universe is unfolding exactly as is intended and that although we, as imperfect humans, can't hope to understand it all at the time, life will generally teach us the lessons we need to learn if we are open to the possibility.

Some people might think that sounds a bit woo-woo. I call it faith. It doesn't have to be faith in a particular god or an organised religion. It can be faith for its own sake: the decision to believe that things will be OK; that this too shall pass.

I have thought about more trivial failures, too. The notable and mortifying occasion, as a seven-year-old on the way to the zoo, that my knickers slipped onto the pavement underneath my skirt because of their loose elastic. There was the first date I went on with my now-boyfriend where, introductions done, I sat down, removed my coat and promptly fell off my chair in full view of everyone in the trendy open-plan bar.

Then there's my failure to understand Excel spreadsheets or make PowerPoint presentations. My failure to comprehend tax or the American voting system or the offside rule no matter how many times someone explains it. My failure to have read *War and Peace* and my repeated failure to find nature documentaries as interesting as everyone else does. My failure to like spicy food or to be able to dive into a swimming pool, despite every single one of my exes insisting they would be the one to teach me to do both.

I understand that thinking about failure this much makes me something of an oddball. Many people try not to dwell on the times in their life when things went wrong or when they made avoidable mistakes or the universe dealt them a really rubbish hand. The second half of the twentieth century saw the rise of the positive psychology movement, prompted by the publication in 1952 of Norman Vincent Peale's *The Power of Positive Thinking* (sample quote: 'Believe in yourself! Have faith in your abilities!') and when this merged with the later trend towards self-help, we found ourselves constantly being encouraged to think good thoughts and not indulge the negative, which was, we were confidently informed, holding us back from reaching our full potential. We were told that we needed to start each day with an affirmation spoken directly into the mirror, in the manner of Robert De Niro's character in *Taxi Driver*, except less psychopathic. In return, we were promised wealth, influence, happiness and true love. It turned out that all we had to do was put together an upbeat mood board and success would manifest itself.

It's not that I don't have sympathy with aspects of the positive-thinking movement. I do. You can, for instance, train your brain to be happier (and a portion of this book will be dedicated to telling you how). Being optimistic can indeed give you the impetus you need to do things you might otherwise fear. It's just that all of this requires substantially more effort than talking to yourself in the mirror or collating pseudo-philosophical quotes on Pinterest. Our mental muscles require just as much working out as our physical ones.

The knock-on effect of 'positivity' has been to marginalise failure, as if negativity is as contagious as leprosy; as if to think about it too much means we're consigning ourselves to forever picking over the bones of the past like depressed hyenas.

In our modern age, we are bombarded with success stories to such an extent that we are in danger of believing exceptionalism is the norm. Logically, it can't be so. An exception is an exception precisely because it lies outside the average. And yet we live in an age of curated perfection, where social media encourages us to believe we are all celebrities in our own lives. We are led to think that we deserve success and will be rewarded with it if only we are clever enough or thin enough or tanned enough or famous enough or charitable enough or sociable enough or, in some way, *good* enough.

At the same time, our omnipresent online culture has scared us into believing that any failure will be humiliatingly public. Send out an ill-thought-through Tweet one day and you could become a viral internet sensation the next for all the wrong reasons. As a result, we have become more averse to risk or experimentation, for fear that any failure will make us seem less than perfect and that our mistakes will be played out in front of a circus of online critics, booing and hissing from behind their toxic avatars.

How can we be happy in this scenario? It is not enough just to think it into being. We have been taught to pursue happiness as the ultimate goal. But happiness is, by necessity, transient. It can only be fully appreciated in opposition to other, darker emotions. Living in a constant state of peak happiness would be exhausting – a bit like perpetually being on the fastest bit of a rollercoaster. It might be fun, but it's high-octane and unpredictable and, by the end of it, your hair looks really bad. What if the worthier goal is the quieter, less glamorous contentment? What if, instead, we sought to nurture an acceptance that difficult things will happen as well as great things and that there is much to be learned from experiencing both? Of course, that thinking process requires effort and practice. It doesn't just happen. But this book will offer you ways of incorporating it into your daily routines.

So, yes, I have spent a large portion of the last couple of years thinking incessantly about failure, and the weird thing is that it hasn't been a negative experience. On the contrary, I feel stronger, happier and more empowered as a result. I'm no longer embarrassed by my mistakes because when I look back at the biggest moments of crisis in my life, I now feel proud of my resilience in surviving them. They have made me who I am, but they do not define me.

If we learn about our past, and ask what it is trying to teach us, then we are no longer condemned to repeat it. Embracing failure is embracing growth. Failure happens to us all, even those celebrity success stories who appear like shimmering modern gods on the red carpet and who seem to have everything sorted.

Failure does not see status – although, admittedly, wealth and privilege make some failures conspicuously easier to bear. But on the whole, it is a democratising force – and that's curiously liberating. If you know something is going to happen, then why spend your life trying to avoid it? Why not accept the fact of failure and endeavour to turn it to your advantage where possible? And why not discuss it? The only way to tackle taboos is to talk about them. Our antidote to shame is shared experience, which is why we should all be more open when things go wrong. When you destigmatise failure, it loses its power to harm you.

That's where Failosophy comes in.

Failosophy brings together all the lessons I've learned from my own life, from hosting the podcast and interviewing a series of brilliant, stimulating people and from meeting many wonderful readers and listeners who have been kind enough to share their stories with me. I have distilled all this precious material into seven key principles of failure. These are not exhaustive, nor will every single one hold equal resonance for everyone's personal situation. The principles are intended as helpful guides through life's rough patches. Consider them the equivalent of having a chat with a good friend who wants to make you feel better. The advice is practical but, I hope, inspirational too. There are carefully selected quotes from my guests who have insights into everything from failed exams and romantic break-ups to how to cope with severe anxiety. You will meet Malcolm Gladwell, Alain de Botton, Phoebe Waller-Bridge, Lemn Sissay, Nigel Slater, Emeli Sandé, Meera Syal, Dame Kelly Holmes, Andrew Scott and many, many more within these pages. You will hear from footballers, psychotherapists, politicians, pop stars, chefs and former reality TV contestants.

There are some caveats. Firstly, it's important to state that I am not fetishising failure. Nor am I suggesting you actively pursue it, pinning evidence of your terrible decisions proudly to your chest like war medals. I'm an advocate of trying your hardest at any given task but, if having tried your best, you still fail, my point is that this does not, in itself, mean that the failure has to be life-defining. However difficult it might seem at the time, it is possible to learn something necessary as a result of most failures.

Secondly, I am not claiming that my way works for everyone. You must feel free to do whatever you want with *your* failures! If that means sitting with a failure, not wanting to take any sort of positives from your experience of it, that's absolutely fine. It's simply that I choose a different path. I choose to believe something good can come from almost everything, even if we can't instantly make out what that positive is. Sometimes, you can only know that with hindsight.

Thirdly, not every failure can be easily assimilated. I am aware that I speak from a position of extreme privilege: I am white, middle-class and have a roof over my head. I cannot write from personal experience about what it is like to be a woman of colour, a marginalised person, someone who is homeless or living with a chronic illness or addiction. But many of my podcast guests can, and that is why I include them here.

Some failures are far more traumatic than others. I'm not saying that we can all bounce back immediately with smiles on our faces at every juncture. There will, in specific instances, be a necessary period of grieving. It's important to allow that process the time it needs before doing anything else. You don't have to feel better immediately. There is no such thing as failing at failing. It's also important to know that there is no hierarchy of distress. If you feel pain, that pain is a fact, whatever the cause of it.

But there is a difference between pain and suffering, between the event and the victimhood. Pain, like failure, happens to us all. We accidentally burn our tongue on a cup of tea that is too hot. There is the immediate pain, which hopefully subsides quite quickly. Then there is the subsequent suffering, which lasts a bit longer as we struggle to taste food for a few days. But imagine beating yourself up about the fact that you'd been stupid enough to burn your tongue for several weeks and months afterwards? That would be prolonging suffering unnecessarily. Instead, you could say to yourself 'Well, I burned my tongue, but at least I'll know for the next time to add a bit of cool water to my tea before I drink it.'

That, in a nutshell, is Failosophy. But this book will concern itself with more than just tea, I promise. Read it all in one go, or dip into relevant sections whenever you encounter failure in a specific part of your life. Either way, I hope it might help you to realise that failure does not have to be alienating. In truth, it is the opposite: it connects us all. It makes us human.

What Is Failure?

'Mistakes are, after all, the foundations of truth
and if a man does not know what a thing is,
it is at least an increase in knowledge if he
knows what is not'

CARL JUNG, PSYCHOANALYST

What is failure? Great question. It was one I deliberately avoided answering for a while, because it seemed such a hard thing to explain. But eventually the definition I came up with was that failure is what happens when something doesn't go according to plan. So then you have to start questioning the plan – where did you get it from? Did someone tell you this was the right way to be? Was it an overly critical parent or a judgemental former partner? Is it social conditioning that's making you believe you're not at the right place in your life? Is it your own internal critical voice? Or is it that you've watched too many 1980s rom-coms and you think that everything has a happy ending, preferably accompanied by an uplifting musical montage? (This isn't entirely a joke: I realised in my late thirties that my idea of romantic love had mostly come from an intravenous cultural drip of *Sleepless in Seattle*, *Pretty Woman* and *Working Girl*. It wasn't helpful. They are great films, but they should not be adopted as how-to guides for life unless you want to end up as a secretarial prostitute with a penchant for late-night radio phone-in shows.)

Once you start dismantling the 'plan' you had for yourself, you come to realise that the failure to stick to it might not be as wounding as you first imagined. Plans, after all, are an objective solution to a subjective problem: you can't, with any reliability, plan to be somewhere in five years' time because you simply don't know what will happen in those intervening years – and I go into this concept in more detail with Failure Principle number 6: 'There is no such thing as a future you.'

The problem with my definition of failure is that it doesn't fully tackle those cataclysmic life events that cannot be easily explained. As I was writing this book, Clemmie, one of my closest friends, had a brain haemorrhage and a massive stroke at the age of 38. Briefly, it looked as though she might not survive. If she did, her family was told, she would be in a dramatically altered state. In defiance of medical expectation, Clemmie not only survived but exceeded every single prediction made of her. She underwent major brain surgery, then had to re-learn how to walk and talk. Her courage and her love of life in this, the most extreme of circumstances, was a privilege to behold.

While she was in a rehabilitation hospital, undergoing strenuous days of back-to-back physical, occupational and speech therapy sessions, there was an outbreak of COVID-19. It rapidly became a global pandemic, affecting us all. Outside visitors were banned from the hospital in order to protect the patients. Across the world, people were dying, cities were going into lockdown and families were putting themselves in self-isolation. Life seemed suddenly to contract. And Clemmie was having to endure the toughest battle of her life without seeing her husband or her two young children.

Shortly after undergoing a cranioplasty to replace half of her skull, Clemmie was diagnosed with COVID-19 too (she was the first patient in the hospital to test positive which, I joked with her, was just typical given her history of over-achievement). So now, as well as having to recover from a stroke and brain surgery, she also had to contend with a life-threatening virus no one really understood. She was ill, exhausted and isolated from her loved ones. Her daily sessions of work continued with the therapists wearing hazmat suits and face masks.

Not once did Clemmie utter a single word of complaint. She told me, time and again, that she had chosen life, and was grateful for having been given that chance. It was extraordinary to see the monumental power of her strength up close. In the end, she was discharged from hospital less than three months after her stroke.

Her husband sent us a photo of the moment he met her, as she walked through the hospital doors unaided, her shaved head making her look like a rock star. She was wearing a T-shirt emblazoned with the words 'Choose Love'.

I read this passage to Clemmie before putting it into the book. She wanted me to make clear that, even now, her recovery is not complete – it's still difficult for her to shape the right words to express herself, even though she knows exactly what it is she wants to say, and there is still some way to go with her physical therapy. There is, she said, a long road ahead.

I have no doubt that she can do it because, well, it's her we're talking about. I don't think I've ever witnessed such a display of grace, dignity or courage in the face of a seemingly insurmountable struggle. She never questioned the unfairness of it.

But although Clemmie never asked 'Why me?', I know that I did on her behalf. Why her? There was never a satisfactory answer.

It would be impossible to equate these life-altering episodes with, say, a failure to pass an exam. And it would be monstrous to say that there was any sort of mystical explanation for them. The truth is, I don't know why bad things happen to good people. But I do know that the human spirit has an extraordinary ability to withstand and survive.

I recently went on a promotional tour to Amsterdam, where I was interviewed by a journalist who told me that the Dutch have two words for failure. One is *fale*, which applies to your common-or-garden variety failures, such as failing a job interview or failing to get into university. The other is *pech*, which means a failure that is beyond our control, a rupture caused by existential bad luck which is not our fault. It has the same etymological root as the English word 'pitch', meaning dark or black – a term that derives from the sticky brown substance left over after the distillation of wood tar or turpentine. Pitch was used in the sixteenth century to waterproof ships. The writer Daniel Defoe used the phrase 'pitch-dark' to describe a hurricane in 1704. The concept of *pech* helps us to understand that failure can also be a state of unexplained darkness, in which it is sometimes difficult to see any crack of light.

For anyone who finds themselves in the grip of that sort of failure, there is little to be done to attack the failure itself. But perhaps we do have the power, however small, to shape our processing of, and our reaction to, times of crisis. Perhaps we can waterproof our sailing ships so that they are better equipped for the next thunderstorm.

That, in any case, is my hope.

The Seven Failure Principles

'You don't have to be the best, just try your best'

MABEL, POP STAR

'The difference between hope and despair is a
different way of telling a story from the same facts'

ALAIN DE BOTTON, PHILOSOPHER

After a few months of recording and editing podcast
episodes, I began to realise there were certain recurring
themes that kept cropping up and certain pieces of advice
or insight that I would hear and think, 'Wow, that's so
helpful. I'll have to write that down.'

At first, I thought there were five Failure Principles,
but as time went on, I realised there were actually seven.
Ask me in a couple of years, and there will probably
be 21, but for now, these seem fairly comprehensive.

1. Failure just is

This might sound obvious. Bear with me.

The first failure principle starts with acknowledging that failure is a fact. It exists. Like oxygen. You can't wish oxygen away or live your life trying to avoid it because that would be stupid and impossible. Oxygen is integral to our survival and so, in its own way, is failure. Failure gives us the opportunity to learn, if we choose to let it. You have to make the mistake in order to solve the problem.

Failure has happened to all of us and it will continue to happen to all of us at various points in our life. Once you realise this, it becomes a great leveller. There is nothing at all, on this whole, wide, unique, fertile planet that can insulate us from failure forever. There just isn't. Wishing it were otherwise is like wishing away oxygen. Or anything else that exists as a fact: teabags, for instance, or shoelaces. There's no point living your life in fear of teabags or shoelaces, just as there is no point living your life in fear of failure.

Failure is a fact. The emotion we attach to it is separate and, to a greater or lesser extent, within our control.

Failure is also not what other people tell you it is. Your experience of failure is personal. As much as possible, it should exist separately from the judgement of others.

'The fact of worrying about whether it's all going wrong is pointless. What it should be about is just thinking, "Well, all I can do is the best I can do, in the way I think is the best way, and we'll see what happens at the end" … Failure is part of the process of getting where you need to be'

– ANDY MCNAB, AUTHOR
AND FORMER SAS SOLDIER

Other people's perceptions are skewed by their own emotional, cultural, familial and professional baggage and are not always going to be the best marker of how you should live your life. As difficult as that sounds, in this age of aggregating likes and double-taps, try as much as possible to untangle your feelings about failure from anyone else's assessment of it.

I was taught to observe failure by Haemin Sunim, a South Korean Buddhist 'mega-monk' (he's referred to as a 'mega-monk' because he has over a million followers on Twitter and the *Guardian* decided to call him that in a headline). As a mega-monk, Sunim is one of the most influential Zen Buddhist teachers in the world. His name means 'nimble wisdom'.

When I met him in January 2019 at his publisher's office in central London to record the podcast, he struck me as someone who was uninterested in small talk. He was dressed in unassuming monastic garb: a modest quilted grey overcoat worn belted around some equally modest grey trousers, and he seemed so self-contained that my inconsequential chatter about the weather felt embarrassingly over the top. I was trying so hard to break the ice, I hadn't realised there was no ice to be broken. I didn't need to try. I could just be.

Still, for the first few questions after I started recording with Sunim, I panicked. He left such long pauses before answering that I worried he had taken offence at something I'd said or simply wasn't going to answer at all.

'It took me a long time to realise that I can't change other people. And I can't actually control other people. I don't control what they do. I can only control myself'

– TARA WESTOVER, AUTHOR

'The minute you let go of the fear of failure, you score more'

– ENIOLA ALUKO, FORMER
ENGLAND WOMEN'S
FOOTBALLER

'Putting my failures down on paper, or even talking about them – it doesn't banish them. They're still there. But it makes me realise that it wasn't the end of the world and, if anything, possibly some good has come out of it'

– NIGEL SLATER, COOK AND AUTHOR

Then, when he did speak, he would do so with such concision that I rapidly found myself burning through all my pre-prepared questions and running out of things to ask. He felt no need to fill a silence.

After a while, I got used to his rhythm. It was calming. My internal neurotic chatter began to quieten itself. What he was doing, I now realise, was allowing space for us both to contemplate what had just been said and what was about to be said. We were observing before we were reacting.

This, said Sunim, was the key to greater understanding. The whole point of meditation, he told me, was 'to become aware of what's happening in your mind. It is not to get somewhere, [to] some kind of peaceful inner state. Rather, it is whether you can become aware of what is really happening in your mind, clearly. That is precisely what you're supposed to do.'

So, I asked, is the next step to observe that but not to attach emotion to it?

'Right,' he said. 'If you are attaching some emotion or expectation then you become mindful [of that]: "Oh, I'm expecting something wonderful to happen. But it's not happening. I feel like a failure."'

The key to meditation, he continued, is 'to see yourself objectively in a non-judgemental way: *that's* the meditation.'

It's the same thing, I believe, with failure. The key is to start by seeing it objectively, in a non-judgemental, un-fearful way. It is to contemplate the fact of it before attaching any kind of feeling to your perception of it. Perceptions and feelings can often be warped and unhelpful. They can arise from panic, grief, disappointment and internal criticism. In a time of crisis, they are often not the best or most reliable measure of what is actually happening. These negative feelings will sometimes give us the wrong advice because they are automatic reflexes, hardwired in us from past experiences that might no longer be relevant to our current situation. Often, we feel we have to resist what is happening, to chafe against it and pretend it isn't so. But this never works.

'Whenever we feel very unhappy it is because we are resisting what is,' Sunim continued. 'Whenever we resist what is, then of course we'll feel very unhappy. The trick is how do we turn our mind and then try to accept the thing as it is?

'We will fail. The question is whether we can fail gracefully and also whether we can learn something from that experience.'

Sunim taught me that instead of being tortured by the feelings you have around failure, the simple act of observation is a form of meditation. Who is it doing the observing, Sunim asked? It is you, he concluded, a separate being that can observe your emotions rather than be consumed by them. And it is you – that essential, enlightened, observational being – who is in control of what happens next.

'Success is a personal
perception'

– JESSIE BURTON, AUTHOR

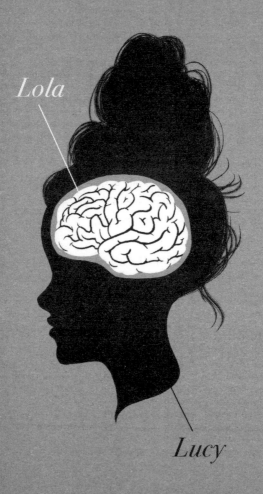

Lola

Lucy

2. You are not your worst thoughts

If we exist separately from our thoughts, the impact of this is seismic. Imagine switching off all of your thoughts, one by one – the worry about having left the oven on this morning; the concern about whether your child is doing well enough at school; the nagging feeling that you should have called your mother; the decision about what you're going to have for dinner – would you still exist?

The answer is yes. If we turn off our thoughts, there is still an 'us' there.

In the past, I used to set great store by external markers of success: getting good exam results and job promotions. In this manner, I believed I would prove myself worthy of love and approval. It was my way, I suppose, of shoring up a lack of self-esteem.

I thought that if I did everything right, no one would ever be able to dislike me for having done something wrong. And if no one else disliked me, I couldn't logically dislike myself. Doing things well was, I thought, necessary proof of my existence. It was the price I paid for admission into the theme park called life.

Yet it never seemed to work. The thrill that a good result or job appraisal gave me was temporary.

'I think every human being
has the inalienable right to
live and decide what rules
work for them'

– JAMES FREY, AUTHOR

It didn't protect me from heartache or loss or abandonment or being terrible at team sports. It didn't protect me from the failure I was trying so hard to avoid. It didn't make me feel that much stronger or more certain about who I was. Instead, all it did was to confuse who I was with the things I did.

Gradually, I learned that intellectual box-ticking is often an external response to an internal lack. I began to realise that if I never achieved anything outwardly ever again, I would still exist. The voice in my head is not who I am. Rather, as Sunim had taught me, I am the one capable of observing it.

Once we deconstruct the external idea of self – those projections that are reflected back on us by the demands and the expectations of the outside world – we are left with an internal self that requires nothing extra in order to be. Its presence is enough.

And here's the best bit: the act of simply being connects us to others in a fundamental way because we are no longer disguising ourselves in the continuous effort to be 'better' than we really are. We aren't pretending. We are our authentic, congruent, integrity-filled selves, where our internal and our external aspects are one and the same. That makes us more comfortable to be around. Instead of being the guest at a party who is constantly attempting to one-up the other invitees, we can be the person who is at peace with who they are and doesn't have to show off to be thought worthy. Who wouldn't rather be *that* dude?

That's the theory, at least. Putting it into practice is harder.

This is where Mo Gawdat comes in. Gawdat is the former chief business officer of Google X, the so-called moonshot factory where they invent apparently crazy ideas like a balloon-powered internet. He is also one of my most downloaded podcast guests of all time. His interview aired in April 2019 and at almost every event I've spoken at since, at least one person will tell me that 'the Mo Gawdat episode changed my life'. I know what they mean. It changed mine too.

When Gawdat came on *How To Fail With Elizabeth Day*, he talked about his firmly held belief that everyone could be happy if they chose to be. He based this on his own experiences. In his late thirties, on paper Gawdat had everything he could have desired: a flourishing career, money, a loving wife, two wonderful children and a taste for expensive cars.

'I bought Rolls-Royces,' he told me. 'There was a time where my garage had 16 cars in it. You would buy one, you would sit in it, you would feel a jolt of happiness for around 60 seconds, then you start to drive and what do you see? You see the road. You hear a little jiggle on the side of the car and you just, again, go, "That's not the right one. Maybe another one is going to make me happy."'

Despite his material wealth and his family life, Gawdat was unhappy. No matter how many cars he bought,

'I took being perfect so, so
seriously because I couldn't
trust myself to still love myself
if I made a mistake'

– CAMILLA THURLOW,
CAMPAIGNER AND FORMER
REALITY TV CONTESTANT

he was still depressed. And so, like the engineer he was, he decided to approach his unhappiness as a scientific problem. For 12 years, he applied all his analytical skill into devising a solution. The result was an equation for happiness, outlined in his international bestseller, *Solve for Happy*.

The equation states simply that happiness is greater than or equal to your perception of the events in your life minus your expectation of how life should be. Essentially, if you expect nothing, you can't be disappointed. Whereas if you expect too much, you'll always feel dissatisfied.

To put this theory into practice, Gawdat said, you had to accept that your brain is an organ you have the ability to control. Your thoughts are a biological product of your brain in much the same way that the blood pumped around your body is a biological product of your heart. You are not your blood. You are also not your thoughts. So it is entirely reasonable for you to stop your brain getting carried away with the panicked, anxious responses it uses to deal with confusion.

Don't get me wrong. Our brains are sophisticated and useful things when they're offering up solutions based on thinking that's insightful ('should we look at this differently?') or experiential ('what do I know of the world that will help?'). Our brains are less helpful when they get stuck on a loop of incessant chatter because we're stressed and over-adrenalised after our eighth cup of coffee in as many hours. In these situations, our brain can sometimes misread the panicked signals our body is sending it as more threatening than they actually are.

Gawdat gave the example of when he'd had an argument with his daughter, Aya. Afterwards, he found himself walking away 'and the first thing that comes to my brain is, "Aya doesn't love you any more." I literally stopped in the middle of the street and said, "What did you just say? How can you come up with that pain? Where did that come from, brain? Why are you telling me this? Do you have evidence for what you're telling me?" Basically, is your brain really that reliable if you let it loose? Or does it take us to places that make us unhappy and make us suffer for no reason whatsoever?'

Gawdat believes that, if you are neurologically healthy and of sound mind, you can train your brain to think more positively. You can ask it to take a negative thought and replace it with a positive one; it's simply a matter of practising.

'You tell your brain to raise your left hand. Have you ever had your brain come back to you and say, "Oh no, no, no. I'd prefer to raise my left foot"? No,' he continued, 'your brain does what you tell it to do.

'Now, here's the trick. I call my brain Becky, OK? – if you have a friend in school, Becky, who was so annoying that she showed up every seven minutes, told you awful things about yourself, made you feel horrible and then left with no positive impact whatsoever on your life, would you wake up the next morning, go to school, and say,

"I miss Becky"? Would you listen to Becky when she speaks? What would you do with Becky when she starts to do that? You say, "No, Becky, please don't do this to me." If Becky starts to tell you weird lies you say, "Becky, do you have any evidence to back this up?" If Becky doesn't, Becky is a third party [and] you would say, "Becky, this is crap. You don't have the right to waste my life on crap." And that's exactly what our brains do. I stop in the middle of a conversation and I say to myself, "Becky, what did you just say?"'

In 2014, personal tragedy hit Gawdat's life with shattering force. His beloved son, Ali, died during a routine operation at the age of 21. At this point, Gawdat's conceptual ideas collided with the reality of unimaginable grief. Could he ever be truly happy again?

Five years had passed since Ali's death when I met Gawdat – and still, he said, 'Three to four times a week, I wake up in the morning or I go to bed at night and the only thought that comes to my head is, "Ali died." He is part of my heart. It's just I feel that part of me is missing.'

This is the message his brain still gives him.

'I answer in a very simple way,' Gawdat continued, 'and I say, "Yes, Brain. But Ali also lived."'

'"Ali died" is a horribly painful thought. "Ali lived" is the same thought. But it's a beautiful thought. It's 21 years of joy, of wisdom, of learning, of insightful discoveries, of memories, of him taking care of Aya, taking care of me,

'The primary cause of
unhappiness is never
the situation but your
thoughts about it'

– ECKHART TOLLE,
SPIRITUAL TEACHER

taking care of his mother, that I wouldn't replace for anything. Honestly, even if you tell me, "We will take away your pain for losing your son," I would say, "No, no, no, hold on. I want him. I want the 21 years."

'When I say, "Ali lived" I start to get memories that are all happy, all joyful, all the things that we did together. That's me being the boss. That's me telling my brain to take charge, so that if there is something we can do, we do it. If there isn't, then don't torture me, because there is no point torturing me if there is nothing I can do about it.'

When he stopped talking, I struggled not to cry. The advice he had given was so seismic in its impact, and yet so quiet in its execution.

Our worst thoughts frequently do not tell us the truth. They can be the product of grief or panic or sadness or a historic defence mechanism that has outlived its usefulness. They can assume the voices of harsh parents or disapproving teachers or the perpetual internal critic who cautions us against getting too big for our boots. But what evidence do they have for their assertions? And why would we listen to Becky, the playground pessimist, anyway?

We exist separately from our negative thoughts, and we are in charge of interrogating their validity and of changing the way we speak to ourselves.

Instead of 'Ali died', 'Ali lived'.

Instead of 'this ended', 'it existed'.

It's the same thought but differently expressed. After the pain has been felt, we do not have to dwell in suffering. We can fail, and we can be at peace with our sadness.

Our thoughts can be many things. Let's allow them the space to be beautiful.

3. Almost everyone feels they've failed at their twenties

Out of all the failures my guests have discussed on the podcast, there is one singular, recurring theme. It is not failed driving tests or failing to get into university (although these two come up a lot as well). No, it is the fact that the vast majority of them feel they failed at their twenties.

To begin with, I was surprised by how many of my interviewees – whatever their background, gender or profession – shared this antipathy towards an entire decade. I had imagined that maybe people would choose their teenage years as part of their history of failure because we're culturally conditioned to believe, through hundreds of films, books and sitcoms, that adolescence is the most unbearable and rebellious state of development. But most people I talk to seem to be fine with their teenage years. Now that I think about it, it's probably because that's when they're *expected* to misbehave, so (to use the Mo Gawdat equation) the experience of life as it is, is meeting their expectation of how it should be.

'I failed many times,
massively, in my twenties.
Constantly'

– SAMIN NOSRAT,
TELEVISION CHEF

In your twenties, however, expectation and experience diverge. On the one hand, there's the clichéd idea that we should all be having a thrillingly wild time, out every night with our friends, pursuing a footloose, responsibility-and-hangover-free existence littered with one-night stands, loud music and brightly coloured cocktails served in Martini glasses. These days, we should not only be doing all of this, but we should also be *seen* to be doing it, so that our fun acquires a performative quality which can only exist fully through the prism of other people's refracted gazes.

On the other hand, we're also meant to be pursuing rewarding careers, putting down roots, forging healthy, long-term relationships and ideally saving towards a pension too because we're all going to live to at least 105. For many of us, our twenties will mark our first steps into the world beyond full-time education. For all their shortcomings, school and university at least have structure, timetables and exam results to tell us how we're doing. Adult life is bafflingly free of these signposts. There is no test you can sit to reveal whether you're an A-grade grown-up, there is only what other people seem to be doing – and in the Instagram age, they all seem to be doing far better than we are.

Although social media has given us new ways to curate the appearance of perfection, the need for comparison has always been there. Now it has simply been amplified.

'I just wanted not to be me. I didn't feel cool enough, didn't feel smart enough, didn't feel like I was good enough'

– FEARNE COTTON,
BROADCASTER, PODCASTER
AND AUTHOR, ON HER
TWENTIES

For a younger generation of 20-somethings, who came of age in an era of high rents, a competitive job market and the global insecurity bequeathed by financial crashes, climate change and unpredictable elections, the level of this amplification is almost unbearable. Your twenties are when you forge your identity and work out who you are. Ideally, you'd be able to do that in private. It's much harder when you're stressed about bringing in a decent salary, anxious about making the right life choices and frazzled by the pressure of having to pretend you've got it all sorted by posting pictures of freshly baked vegan chocolate brownies on Instagram at the weekend.

One of the most frequently reproduced inspirational quotes for millennials is 'Dance like nobody's watching', which has been emblazoned on every basement toilet cut-price neon sign and decorative tchotchke since the dawn of modern time. To which I respond: how are you meant to dance like nobody's watching when it feels as if everyone is watching, liking, commenting and judging your music taste? How can you even find time to dance? And what if you're a rubbish dancer? Should you be taking dance lessons at the weekend to improve? Would that make you more dateable, relatable, fit and successful?

It's exhausting. But the people we're comparing ourselves to, the ones who appear to have it all are, in truth, not so very different from the rest of us. They also feel confused in their twenties.

'When you're 20, you should be trying a million things – especially the things you're not good at, just to see if there's some wonderful little thing you can extract from the experience'

– MALCOLM GLADWELL,
AUTHOR

'Your twenties is about finding your identity and finding out who you are. For me, I had no clue who I was really. I thought I did. I thought I knew everything about me, but I knew nothing'

– JAMIE LAING,
ENTREPRENEUR AND
REALITY TV STAR

The broadcaster Fearne Cotton talked about developing bulimia. The memoirist and podcaster Dolly Alderton recalled losing her way as she worked in a TV production job she didn't want. The singer Lily Allen struggled to understand herself in the blinding glare of the limelight and had three children in quick succession, the first of whom was stillborn – a trauma that haunts her still. The author Sebastian Faulks experienced depression in his twenties. The cultural commentator Raven Smith failed to graduate. The actor Andrew Scott dropped out of his university degree. Phoebe Waller-Bridge went on a lot of bad dates (bad dates that later provided inspiration for *Fleabag*, the television comedy she created that became a cultural phenomenon and won six Emmys, two Golden Globes and one BAFTA). The journalist John Crace lost a decade of his life to heroin addiction. The writer Marian Keyes compared her battle with alcoholism in her twenties to 'cycling a stationary bike … except I wasn't because everything was getting worse'.

The more I speak to people about the wilderness of their twenties, the more I realise that perhaps the greatest achievement of this particular decade is living through it. Because here's the thing: all those people who felt like failures in their twenties survived to tell the tale. For many of them, their thirties or forties were far more rewarding. That has certainly been my experience. It turns out that anyone who ever told you that getting older is a wonderful liberation, because you know yourself better and accumulate wisdom as you age, wasn't actually lying. It's true.

'My twenties were hard. I was jelly. I was unfinished and unmoulded, and carrying a lot of baggage and expectation about how I should behave'

– MEERA SYAL, ACTOR, COMEDIAN, PLAYWRIGHT AND AUTHOR

'I'd really like to have the skin from my twenties, but I prefer my heart and guts now'

I'm 41 now, and I have never felt more empowered or more fulfilled. My twenties might not have been my decade, but in a way my thirties were – those were the years in which I published my books and launched a podcast. Having said that, my personal progress back then often did seem out of sync with my peers, who were busy getting married and having babies while I got divorced and had failed IVF, so maybe we can all feel a bit lost in different decades. But we can also appreciate that getting older gives us a deeper pool of self-awareness and experience to draw from, and that this helps us build up the resilience we need to cope with uncertainty.

For this reason, I have high hopes that my forties will be even better than the years that have led up to them. This is what Meera Syal meant when she told me that 'we all ripen at different times'. She was 58 when I interviewed her, and she said that every decade she'd lived through had had a different flavour. What was the flavour of her current decade, I asked?

'Juicy plum,' she replied, without missing a beat. 'I'm ripe and ready to go.'

Many of us who have the privilege of looking back at our twenties feel the same as Syal. We might not all be juicy plums (personally, I think I'm more of a slightly underripe mango) but we can still be grateful for what our twenties taught us at the same time as being thankful they are over.

So, if you feel lost in your particular decade, that you aren't doing what you should be or that other people are succeeding more, better and faster than you, then rest assured that you are not alone. The vast majority of us feel the same. I promise you: simply by living through this particular decade, you are learning valuable lessons about yourself. The juicy plum lies in your future.

4. Break-ups are not a tragedy

'Let everything happen to you
Beauty and terror
Just keep going
No feeling is final'

– RAINER MARIA RILKE, POET

Break-ups are horrible. I know this because I have an extensive evidence base. I've had six serious break-ups, including one divorce, and each one of them has well and truly sucked. Although they get easier to deal with in the sense that I now know what to expect about how I'm going to feel when a relationship ends, it never stops being a gut-wrenching, heart-breaking, soul-sapping immersion into what it means to be fully human.

In the wake of a break-up, I question everything. I question my own judgement for being with someone who ultimately failed to live up to my hopes. I question myself either for not being enough for the other person to love devotedly or for not being able to keep the embers of a dying relationship alive. I question society for the messages it has given me about one-on-one romantic love

'I'm one of those people who equates falling in love with having food poisoning. Please, please, may I never fall in love again'

— NIGEL SLATER, COOK AND AUTHOR

being the only true route to contentment. I question every single heteronormative rom-com I've ever watched and I scowl at every single loved-up couple I see in the street, clogging up the pavement with their nauseating insistence on holding hands. I question whether I'll ever find anyone I want to be with ever again. I question why the best pop songs are always about love, all the sodding time. I question whether I'll be on my own forever and I fear the possibility of choking one morning on a vitamin supplement I'm taking for the express reason of remaining fit, healthy and attractive, only for my dead body to lie undiscovered for weeks.

But every single time, I've survived. And every single time, I've ended up looking back and being actively grateful for the break-up I'd once wished out of existence. As Mo Gawdat put it to me: 'Can you look back at your life and find any of your break-ups that you would tell yourself, "Wow, it would have been wonderful if I was still with that person today?" Most of the time, for most of us, it's a no. Most of the time, six to eight months later we go like, "Wow, how did I put up with this?" …

'The truth is, we live in a world of abundance. If that person leaves, there are probably 3.4999999 billion others that can qualify to have the joy of being with you.'

It's important to remember that although break-ups feel like an acute form of grief, no one has actually died. They are not a tragedy, even if your distorted perception means it seems like that at the time. I do not say this lightly. When I was 24, a beloved ex-boyfriend of mine did die six months after we broke up. That feeling of loss was of a different magnitude.

The philosopher Alain de Botton explained to me that one meaningful way of looking at important relationships in your life – be they romantic or platonic – is that people are brought to you for a reason. The purpose of their interaction with you is to teach you something you need to know. Once this lesson has been taught, sometimes the person in question will move on; or you are the one who decides the time has come to sign off on a particular chapter.

'I think one should be able to say, "I had a fantastic summer with somebody and that was amazing. The things we shared were amazing,"' de Botton said. '"It didn't last 10 years but it was a fantastic summer." We are quite possessive of certain states of mind. We want to own them forever. We should get better at appreciating the passage of them and not try to hold on to them.'

This means that a relationship is not a failure simply because it ends. Sometimes it is a success precisely *because* it has ended, and you have been given the necessary knowledge you need to evolve (even if that knowledge can often only be identified in hindsight). In the same way, a parent raising a child does not consider it a failure when the child leaves home. On the contrary, if they are balanced, reasonable, thoughtful individuals they consider this the natural outcome of successful parenting.

'The loss can be real, but it can still be the right choice'

– TARA WESTOVER, AUTHOR

'The other person has every right to reject you. It doesn't mean you are not good enough. It's just that it wasn't a good fit'

– HAEMIN SUNIM, ZEN BUDDHIST MONK

The secret to a long-lasting relationship is therefore to keep teaching and learning from each other, to allow each other the space to evolve, rather than to waste one's time searching for a mythical soulmate who meets all your many requirements for perfection.

You can apply the same logic to friendships. When a friend passes in and out of your life, it may be because that friend was intended for a specific phase of existence. Your friend might have brought you comfort in a time of need just as they might have processed some of their own emotional in-tray through their relationship with you. There was an overlap in time, where two complicated humans brought with them all their own fragilities and insecurities and boldly stepped into the central section of a Venn diagram of interests and feelings, and for those moments you served an irreplaceable function for each other. It's OK to let that go. It's OK for the other person to move on once you have both been able to grow.

The actor Andrew Scott touched on this when he spoke about his dislike of the term 'casual sex'. He felt it implied something shameful and transient and ultimately meaningless.

'You can have incredibly potent life-long effects from meeting someone over two weeks, or one week, or, you know, three hours,' he explained. 'You can go, "Oh my God, I learned something." And I think if you're going through that situation where you're having casual sex with people, sometimes that's what you need to do. What was

'I look back and I go, "What an idiot." But it's great because I've learned from it and I'll never do it again'

– VICKY MCCLURE, ACTOR

really important for me was understanding my own sexuality or who you are or what you like. It's such a taboo really. And you have to make mistakes and you have to find out who you are.'

That's the nub of it: break-ups give us a crash-course in who we really are because when a relationship fails, we have to look at what part we had to play in its demise.

I can only speak from personal experience, but when I met the man I now love, I had been bruised by a succession of terrible break-ups and dating rejections. My grandiose illusions of romantic love had taken a necessary battering. I was more realistic, perhaps, but also less tolerant in the same way that, as I've grown older, I have dispensed with any guilt I used to feel for abandoning a book I'm not enjoying before I've finished it. I knew what I wanted from a relationship, and I knew how to say that out loud rather than expecting the other person magically to intuit my thoughts. I had, in short, learned the necessary lessons from love.

What I can now admit, is that I could only have got to this point because of, rather than in spite of, the failed attachments I had experienced before. It's true: every single break-up has been worth it.

5. Failure is data acquisition

As we've already learned, one of the fundamental precepts of Failosophy is that we start by removing, as much as we can, the feeling that failure negatively defines us as people. It doesn't. Failure happens. We respond. The nature of our response will determine how we feel about it.

When I started the podcast, I was interested to discover that there was a gender split in how we viewed failure. All the women I contacted for the debut season said that they'd failed so many times, they couldn't possibly whittle it down to just the three incidents of failure I'd asked for. Almost all the men replied to my initial approach by saying they weren't sure they were right for the podcast as they weren't entirely convinced they *had* failed. I was astonished: there were people out there who, when they made mistakes, did not suffer an existential crisis of self? What sorcery was this?

When I came to speak to them, I realised that these men weren't, in truth, being overweeningly arrogant. It was simply that they saw the world differently. If you're lucky enough to be a cis, white, middle-class man, you are still born into a society that is made in your image. It means that if you encounter failure, you are more likely

'Through failure, if you're honest and you see where you've failed, how you've failed, then every time you get a bit stronger'

– GINA MILLER, CAMPAIGNER

to see it as a perfectly overcome-able obstacle on your path to inevitable success. If a woman, or a marginalised person or a person of colour, were to face the same failure, they might instead believe that it was an all-encompassing verdict on who they were. The world is more unkind to those who have a less sure footing in it.

As I carried on doing the podcast, this dynamic shifted. I now have lots of men who are in touch with their failures and willing to explore their vulnerabilities, just as I have many women who rightly believe their claim to space is as valid as anyone else's. But it did make me think. What if, the next time we failed, we imagined the response of the most arrogant, entitled, privileged person of our acquaintance? I guarantee you that they would let the failure bounce off them like hail off a car bonnet. And although I don't advocate their way of doing things, I also wonder whether it might be possible for the most insecure, self-questioning and sensitive ones among us to become just 5 per cent more like this? What if we all started to view failure not as something that sinks us, but as something that can help us rise: a necessary piece of information that will help us take our next step?

To put it another way: a scientist working on a cure for a terrible disease will try out a number of different strategies before hitting on the solution. If an experiment fails, the scientist in question does not automatically think he or she is a failure; instead they acknowledge that the experiment has taught them something extremely useful by not working. They can eliminate the concept that doesn't work and get closer to the one that will.

It's a mindset that can be applied to multiple areas of life. Take dating, for instance. What if, instead of feeling a personal sense of rejection every time we go on a first date and the other person doesn't want to go on a second, we simply treat that as one more piece of necessary information about what isn't right for us? What if, instead of going down a rabbit-hole of self-loathing every time a romantic partner leaves your double-blue-ticked WhatsApp messages unanswered, you think: 'You are clearly not the right person for me. Thank you for eliminating yourself from my enquiries and allowing me to get closer to the person who is'? (I write from experience, by the way: I met my partner on Hinge.)

What if we're cancelling out the stuff that doesn't work, in order to get closer to the thing that does? In certain contexts, then, failure is not something to be avoided. It is something to be actively pursued.

When I interviewed Deborah Frances-White, the host and creator of the highly successful *The Guilty Feminist* podcast, she told me about her early experiences in acting and comedy. She started talking about 'improv', at which point I silently worried we were going to meander into a lengthy segue involving black leotards and Parisian clown school. But what Frances-White told me was extremely pertinent. She said that doing improv on stage in front of

'There's something very
freeing about being willing
to try something that
doesn't work'

– MALCOLM GLADWELL,
AUTHOR

a group of fellow comedians was an intimidating prospect and the two greatest enemies to doing it well were 'fear and ego'. In order to counteract this, her teacher had started every class by getting the participants to shout, 'We suck and we love to fail!' The impact this had was to normalise failure, to remove the fear and to banish the ego. If you go into something expecting to be rubbish and expecting everyone else to be equally bad, there is less space for your pride to be dented. In a group of people who are actively seeking *not* to succeed, humiliation becomes obsolete.

One of the exercises Frances-White remembered from this phase in her life was called 'Seen Enough'. The idea was that an individual would get up on stage and start improvising on their own. The rest of the class would sit and watch. If any audience member became bored by what they were watching, they got up and left the room. The performer on stage had to keep going until the room was empty.

'And at first that sounds horrific,' Frances-White said. 'Of course! It sounds like, "Oh my God, that's your worst nightmare." And for that reason it's absolutely brilliant … [because] all the time you're ruling out what doesn't work … And I remember doing it, going, "I've got something! This is going to keep the audience!" And it became like a process. It wasn't about my individual talent. It was about what processes will keep an audience transfixed.'

Just like our hypothetical scientist, the exercise enabled Frances-White to separate who *she* was from the process of discovering what worked *for* her. Her failure was a means of data acquisition.

Years later, when Frances-White started teaching undergraduate students at the Royal Academy of Dramatic Art in London, she applied the same ideas to auditioning.

'I always used to say, "When you're auditioning, your first year of auditioning out in the real world, you're collecting data. Don't ever go on an audition to get the job, go on the audition to find out how you best do auditions. How do people respond to you if you go in really confidently? How do they respond if you go in a bit tentatively? How do they respond when you really prepare everything? How do you respond when you let yourself kind of be loose in the room? When you don't say too much at the beginning, when you build rapport?"

'And every time you keep this manual, this little diary, because what you're doing in the first year after drama school is getting good at auditioning and discovering what process best works for you.'

By teaching her students that their goal was to acquire data about auditions, rather than getting the part, Frances-White had removed their fear and their ego. The knock-on effect was that many of her students ended up getting the parts anyway because they felt no pressure.

'It's not going to be plain sailing all the time, especially if you want to be somebody great. You have to be prepared to fail sometimes'

– ENIOLA ALUKO, FORMER ENGLAND WOMEN'S FOOTBALLER

If we are able, as much as possible, to remove both fear and ego when we encounter crisis, we will see failure more clearly for what it is: not as something that defines us, but as a missing piece of knowledge that helps us come closer to completing the jigsaw puzzle of who we truly are.

6. There is no such thing as a future you

'It's nice to have plans, but even a plan C, D and E sometimes doesn't cover the unexpected. So being open to the opportunities that can come, and to roll with them, is really important'

— MEERA SYAL, ACTOR, COMEDIAN,
PLAYWRIGHT AND AUTHOR

I used to be someone with a five-year plan. My plan would be a thing of infinite and varied detail and beauty. I would know where I would be living, what job I'd be pursuing, who I'd be dating and the precise brand of coffee I would drink every morning before going to work.

There was only one problem: the plan never worked.

As much as I liked to imagine myself into the future, I never entirely could. By the time I got to that projected five-year point, I was never quite the person I had thought I would be. I would be living in a different country. I'd be dating someone unsuitable. I'd have given up drinking coffee altogether.

After a while, I realised that instead of reassuring me and giving me clear strategic focus, my five-year plans

'We change and we grow
all the time'

– PHILIPPA PERRY,
PSYCHOTHERAPIST AND
AUTHOR

were actually making me feel like a failure for not living up to my own expectations. I was setting my standards far too high, and I was inevitably disappointed when I didn't achieve them in the allotted and arbitrary time span I had chosen. As we have already learned, overblown expectation is the thief of happiness. If we expect too much of ourselves, we are destined to feel like failures.

It's partly why I don't like New Year's resolutions. We live in a culture that celebrates impossible perfection. We are repeatedly fed the lie that aspiration and ambition can only ever be grounded in our lust for unobtainable things – new cars, new clothes, new homes, new selves – when, in fact, we can motivate ourselves in a different way, by seeking to find contentment in the expression of our truest selves as we already are. We can be happy by learning to live with – and even honouring – our imperfections. They do not always need eradicating. We do not need to buy something to make them disappear.

The falsehood that we must constantly be on a quest to perfect ourselves is pervasive. It encourages us to think of the end of the year as a time of reassessment. On 31 December, we are bloated from a festive season of excess and exhausted from the emotional effort of processing the intensity of the preceding 12 months, and our natural inclination is to want better. We imagine ourselves emerging, transformed and resplendent, into the new year. Shops are selling self-help guides by the dozen, each one promising a new way of constructing a new you.

Sunday newspaper supplements proselytise revolutionary detox plans that promise younger skin, glossier hair and a renewed sense of vigour. The Christmas food leftovers have been replaced by juice cleanses and celery sticks. Everyone seems to take up running.

Into this febrile atmosphere, we unleash the beast of our own self-hatred. We decide to make New Year's resolutions. It's an admirable concept, but by now we feel so hidebound with shame and internalised criticism, that the only resolutions worth making seem to be overly dramatic ones. So we resolve to run marathons even though we don't much like running and still have that one dodgy ankle from the time we fell over drunk during freshers' week. We decide to become vegan, even though we really, really like cheese. We set ourselves the task of learning new languages or instruments or life-drawing techniques because we have suddenly realised there is no more time to waste and, besides, when the clock strikes midnight and it's 1 January, we will be better versions of ourselves, thinking more clearly and with oodles more disposable time in our diaries.

That's the theory, anyway.

Of course, it never turns out like that. After a few weeks, the new running shoes lie untouched by the front door, haunting us with their unspoken judgement as we recover from a torn hamstring. The Italian lessons never work out because we can't seem to find the time to memorise the necessary vocabulary lists. The vegan diet contains a lot of tofu, which turns out to be more expensive than we thought. And so on. We have made ourselves look like failures in our mind's eye simply because the original plan was faulty. In the rush to achieve illusory perfection, we have ignored our own limitations and tried to do too much.

But what if we were to readjust the expectation and tell ourselves that, instead of running a marathon, we would commit to going for a jog when we felt like it? What if, instead of planning for a future version of yourself that doesn't exist, you pay attention to the present you; the one who does?

The American author Kristen Roupenian talked to me about this when I interviewed her for a live recording of the podcast. We had just chatted about how difficult it can be to navigate your twenties, so I asked her what her thirties were proving to be like.

'They've been really good,' she replied. 'It was funny because I was so scared of them. In some ways, it was one of the things that made my twenties hard – I had this timeline that I had imagined for myself that had set points. I think that's super common, to the point where it's a cliché, where you're like, "I want these things by this year and if I don't [get them] I don't even know, it's too terrible to think about, I'll just be a failure for the rest of my life."

'And what happened was I got into my thirties and I had the deadlines I had set for myself just flying away left and right.'

One of the specific things Roupenian had imagined for herself was that she would have a child by the age of 32 and would be happily married to a man, living in their own home. By the time she got to 32, Roupenian had realised that 'not only did I not have a child, but I realised I didn't want one. I had imagined a 32-year-old version of me who would *only* be happy with a husband and a baby and a house. And I worked really hard to get things in order for that future self because I thought she would hate me if I didn't get there. I remember feeling when a relationship would end or something would go wrong, I'd be like, "Oh man, you're going to look back at this when you're 32 and you're going to be like, '24-year-old Kristen, why didn't you take that job?'" I just imagined this total meanie looking back and shaking her finger.

'And then I turned 32 and I was still myself and I didn't want any of the things that I had imagined this rando was going to want. I wanted the same things I had wanted before and I could get them. And that was amazing! That story sort of fell away. It became really clear that I thought I wanted a lot of things I didn't actually want and I had just been telling myself all these stories about what would make Future Me happy, to the point where I was ignoring what present Kristen actually wanted and in fact could have.'

I told her that was the best description of my own psyche that I had ever heard. Plus it was interesting that although the projected 32-year-old Kristen thought she would have a baby and a husband, it turned out that by the time she got to that age, she had a girlfriend and an unbelievable career instead. When I asked whether she still imagined a future self, Roupenian replied that she did, but in a subtly altered way.

'It just feels like I'm imagining *myself* in the future in the way that I just didn't [before]. I don't know why. I just invented this other person to try and please for no reason. I don't know necessarily what I want next year but I feel like, "OK, I know what I want right now and I can sort of extrapolate." I can make a reasonable guess and that seems fine. It's so different.'

What I found so compelling about the way Roupenian explained this state of mind was that the future Kristen she had imagined bore very little connection to the Kristen she actually was. These were the goals that *society* had told her she wanted, rather than the things that felt congruent with her true self. For me, that is the crucial difference. I'm not saying that you should never think about the future; rather that your thoughts about the future should be realistically grounded in the present. Putting aside money for a pension, for instance, is a sensible thing to do because you can take action towards it as your present self. Setting yourself the goal of being a yacht-owning billionaire by the time you're 65 and fixating on this to the extent that you're making yourself feel anxious right now because you're not earning enough money to make this a reality, is a pointless exercise. The

'Things can work out in ways
you can't imagine at the time'

– MISHAL HUSAIN,
BROADCASTER

pension is a less sexy vision than the yacht, I admit, but it's a calmer one too.

The joy of this way of living is that it leaves you space to follow your own passions and instincts when they arise, rather than being constricted by a series of time-sensitive goals you think you have to achieve by a specific point. I probably would never have launched the podcast, or written this book, or learned all this fascinating stuff about failure had I been sticking conscientiously to the original five-year plan of writing novels, getting (and staying) married, buying a house and raising children.

The fact that my marriage ended, that I was unable to conceive and that I did not have a deposit for a house meant that I was able to pursue different things that I thought I might like in the moment – decamping to Los Angeles and living in an Airbnb for three months, for instance. Although the uncertainty felt scary at the time, it also felt liberating. My life felt fluid rather than rigid. Ultimately, these decisions changed the course of my life for the better. Those three months in LA taught me an enormous amount: they made me realise that it was never too late to do something different.

Like Kristen Roupenian, I've come to believe that there is no such thing as a future me. There is the me I am right now, and I need to pay attention to her. That's not to say forward planning is pointless, but unless you can actively contribute something practical towards your future growth right now, there's no point worrying about

'What's next is what's happening right now, where you are in this moment. Your universe will just keep moving the way it moves'

– CUSH JUMBO, ACTOR

the things you can't yet control. You'll deal with your five-year future self when you get to meet her or him. The great possibility of the future lies in one simple fact: it hasn't happened to us yet.

7. Being open about our vulnerabilities is the source of true strength

The most valuable thing I have learned about failure is this: that when we choose to be honest about our own vulnerability, we forge the greatest sense of connection with others and the greatest strength in ourselves. There is solidarity in failure and a courage that comes from the admission of it that feeds into future resilience. Emotional strength, just like its physical equivalent, is a muscle that you build up the more you use it. It isn't always easy. It's often not the thing you want to do. But deciding to face failure head on, to process it and then to learn from it in an honest and open way, is the key to living a more authentic life.

This is a life without pretence, in which you don't have to remember what lies you've told about yourself for fear of being caught out. This is a life in which you don't have to be cooler than you feel, more fashionable than you are or more professionally successful than you know yourself to be. This is a life in which you can be honest about who you are, and where you are respected and loved for your imperfections. Imperfections are what make us human.

'The ability to admit failures is always an expression of strength'

– DAVID BADDIEL,
COMEDIAN, PLAYWRIGHT
AND AUTHOR

'It's OK to say that you're not OK. And by doing that, it alleviates that pressure and you can actually be you a little bit more'

– DAME KELLY HOLMES,
OLYMPIC GOLD MEDALLIST

They are what enable us to relate to each other.

Once you admit your own vulnerabilities and choose to share them, they are no longer fearful things to avoid: the adult equivalent of the bogeyman under the bed. The author and professor Brené Brown has spent years researching the sources of shame and the potential of vulnerability. Shame, she says, can be 'lethal'.

'The less you talk about it, the more you got it,' she explained in a 2013 interview with Oprah Winfrey. The antidote, Brown said, was to talk about it, to connect with another human being about what it felt like.

'Shame depends on me buying into the belief that I'm alone,' Brown continued. 'Shame cannot survive being spoken. It cannot survive empathy.'

It is the same with failure. If we feel ashamed of something that has gone wrong, or defined negatively by a mistake we have made, the antidote is openness. It's always a surprise to discover how many other people have felt the same way.

This has certainly been true for me. When I started talking openly about my failures – infertility, divorce, miscarriage – I found that many people I knew had gone through something similar but had never felt able to speak about it. They had been scared or worried or intimidated by the prospect of breaking a taboo, and yet when we shared our stories with each other, we found comfort in the mutual experience. This process has genuinely made my life more meaningful. I now face any failure armed with the knowledge that I can speak up about things that have happened to me and, in doing so, hopefully help others to remove the burden of their shame or the stigma of their loneliness.

This is why some of my favourite podcast interviews have been with people who are willing to be open about the darkest times in their life. There are four in particular that stick in the mind. The first deals with addiction. The second with a loveless childhood. The third with what it's like to live with severe anxiety. And the fourth? We'll come onto that.

When John Crace, the author and *Guardian* journalist, appeared on the podcast in April 2019, he talked to me about the decade he lost to heroin addiction. He recalled the moment he knew he had to quit, when his wife said, 'You're killing yourself. This has got to stop.'

'That was actually the moment when things began to change because it was at that moment that I realised that I wanted to live more than I wanted to die,' he said, speaking in the front room of his south London home, surrounded by crowded bookshelves and the occasional meowing from the family cat. 'Because in the last six months of my addiction, I had taken to sort of overdosing, once, sometimes twice a week. Not as an act of bravado or even as an act of stupidity, really. It was more of an act of just not caring, of wanting the state of nothingness really, to nullify my life completely. I mean, it's weird because it's all well over 30 years ago and yet talking

'The more honest I am, and the more I put out that is authentically me, the less fear I have'

– FEARNE COTTON,
BROADCASTER, PODCASTER
AND AUTHOR

about it really brings it home. I can feel the sadness inside at the moment. I still feel quite tearful.'

Some months later, when I interviewed the poet Lemn Sissay, he talked about a childhood pockmarked by emotional abuse. Sissay's mother was an Ethiopian student who arrived in England to attend a Christian college in 1966. She was pregnant and unmarried. Shortly after her son was born in 1967, he was taken away from her and placed with a foster family who adopted him against his birth mother's wishes. A social worker re-named him Norman and Sissay grew up in a white, working-class, deeply religious family in Lancashire. His foster parents went on to have three more children. Tensions mounted.

At the age of 12, to his profound confusion, Sissay's foster family placed him in a children's home and said they would never contact him again. He would spend the next five years in a succession of brutal institutions during which he had a mental breakdown. In these dark times, the light of his poetry began to form.

'I felt in many ways I was being taught how to feel worthless,' Sissay said. 'And I was being taught that I was slowly becoming invisible because I wasn't seen. I would be punished if I did something wrong but I wouldn't be congratulated if I did something right. So, for example, the first thing that I wanted in the children's home was a hug. And I didn't get hugged. I stopped being touched at 12. But if I did something wrong, the police would be called, or if I ran away, the police would be called. So I found myself in an institution that was based on whether I followed the rules. But in so doing, I was invisible. It was like, no, you follow these rules but there is no endgame. There's no love at the end of that, there's no hug. Without love, for a child to be told to follow any rules, it's like an emotional fascism.'

After both of these episodes went live, I was inundated with messages and emails from listeners who told me that Crace and Sissay's honesty had made them feel less alone. Many of them were dealing with similar issues and, although they had never met either guest, simply knowing of their existence gave them both comfort and hope.

But the only time I've ever been stopped in Sainsbury's by a stranger who wanted to tell me how much a podcast episode had helped them was after my interview with Camilla Thurlow, the broadcaster, charity campaigner and former *Love Island* contestant. I had been following Thurlow for some time on social media and had watched the 2017 series of *Love Island* on which she had been the runner-up. I had been impressed by the way she handled herself on reality television, intrigued by her former life as an explosive ordinance disposal expert and I had liked the cut of her jib on social media. So I slid into her DMs and asked if she'd come on *How To Fail*. To her credit, Thurlow agreed and sent me three beautifully expressed failures over email, the explanation for each running to several pages.

She turned up to my flat in north London in the summer of 2019, a small, elegant figure clutching an orchid and a bottle of champagne for me (she is a very lovely person) and a huge can of energy drink for herself that seemed almost bigger than she was. She had just recovered from a bout of food poisoning, she explained, hence the need for caffeine.

When we started recording, she revealed that one of her failures was 'not living up to Camilla Thurlow' – the idea of her that people had from watching her on television, rather than the real person she actually was, who often struggled with anxiety and feelings of self-doubt.

'Two things happen and one of them is kind of acute,' she said, sipping on her energy drink. 'So if I go to an event or anything … I always get anxious before events, I always find them difficult, whether they're public events or personal events, I just really worry. But if I'm in a bad phase, that worry becomes almost paralysing. And then I go into a kind of avoidance technique, but I get panicked. And then I tend to be a bit … not more argumentative, but I'm more likely to react. So sometimes people will come up to you at public events and they'll comment on you or they'll say something about your relationship and things like that and I will be 10 times more sensitive to it and then I react far worse to it.

'But then there's also this kind of constant feeling of unease, just in general. It starts to become unbearable to be inside my own head all the time and yeah, I get completely trapped in it, trapped in a really negative sort of spiral, and I find it … it's hard to talk about this: it's not that the other option becomes any less terrifying, but when life becomes unbearable like that, you do start to think in a different way. It starts to change the way you look at everything. And it's difficult for the people around you as well, and that's the other thing – if you're a people-pleaser, as soon as you start disappointing the people around you because of feeling like that, you're trapped in that again, it's just a constant negative spiral.'

I asked her what she meant when she talked about 'the other option being terrifying'.

'Yeah, I mean … without being … yeah. I mean … I don't know how to say this without being a bit … you start to entertain thoughts of what not being alive would be like. And even if it's just letting that cross your mind or whether it becomes a more serious thought pattern, that's when you realise … it's not that that becomes less scary or less worrying, it's just that you can't see how this feeling is going to go … It's when you can't see a way out. There's no light because you don't think there's light at the end of the tunnel.'

When it went live, the episode with Thurlow rapidly became one of the most downloaded of all time. Her insight into anxiety appeared to strike a chord with a generation of young women and men who had struggled to put how they were feeling into words. One listener emailed me to say she had forwarded the episode to her

'The most personal is the
most universal'

– CHARLY COX, POET

family members so that they would finally understand what went on in her head when she couldn't find the words to communicate with them.

And then, I was tapped on the shoulder in the Sainsbury's cheese aisle by a woman called Alice who had recognised me. She worked in the music industry, she said, where they were told never to react when they saw a famous person walking into the office. But, she said, she had promised herself that she would say hello if she ever ran into me. I was bowled over by this, because it's not like I'm Lady Gaga, is it?

Alice told me that Thurlow's generosity and eloquence had moved her deeply. We hugged. I told her how much it meant to me, and how much it would mean to Camilla when I passed it on. Alice was then able to direct me to the cold meats aisle. I remain grateful for this because it was a very big and confusing Sainsbury's.

But perhaps the clearest example of the strengthening power of vulnerability came, for me, from a man called Jonny Benjamin, who was a podcast guest in January 2019. I had met Benjamin at a Facebook panel some months earlier and had been so struck by his sincerity and generosity of spirit that I knew I had to get him on the podcast. Benjamin had struggled with mental health issues for much of his life. He was eventually diagnosed with schizoaffective disorder at the age of 20 and shortly afterwards, found himself standing on the edge of Waterloo Bridge about to jump. He was so desperate that he genuinely believed that the only way to end his pain was to end his life.

'When I got that diagnosis … it just felt like my world had sort of come to an end,' he said on the podcast. 'I thought, "What's the point?" It was hopeless, it was hopeless. And the hospital I was in, it was hopeless, no one around me was getting any better. When I was in hospital I just got worse. So a month into my stay in the hospital, one day something in my mind almost kind of snapped, I remember, and it was … I can sort of go back there, it was horrible. I just remember being like, "This is … I can't … I cannot do this any more. There is only one way out of this and that is suicide. There is no other way out, there's no other way out to escape from this nightmare." I believed that was going to be the rest of my life in hospital, ill, a burden on my family. And so I made the decision to end my life. This is going to sound awful but I kind of felt a bit liberated. Unless you've been there, I don't think people can understand. But I was in such despair and pain that finally I had a way out and I kind of felt liberated. And so that's what led me to run away from the hospital. I managed to escape. I said I needed a cigarette and they let me out and I ran as fast as I could and ended up on this bridge.'

At this point in the interview, both Jonny and I were in tears. I have always been told, in my work as a journalist, that our job is to remain objective. It is to leave our own emotions out of a situation as much as possible.

'The more you can be vulnerable around failure, the more time you're going to save other people. It's an act of singular generosity'

– ALAIN DE BOTTON,
PHILOSOPHER

It is to remember that this is someone else's story and that we are conduits for it.

And yet, I have grown to believe this guidance is only relevant in certain specific situations. I have been lucky enough to have some deeply meaningful encounters through recording the podcast and the connection I have felt with each and every one of my guests has been profoundly personal. To deny that, I think, is to deny one's own humanity. It is also to deny them the power of their story and a moment of necessary empathy.

Jonny took a breath and continued. What happened next was that a passing stranger noticed his distress and stopped to talk. It was a single act of compassion that saved his life. He stepped back from the edge.

Six years later, Jonny launched an internet campaign to find that stranger. More than 319 million people around the world followed the search until it was picked up by a TV breakfast show which finally reunited Jonny with his Good Samaritan, Neil Laybourn. The two of them now tour the country talking about mental health in schools and workplaces. In 2016, Jonny was awarded an MBE for his work.

When Jonny told his story, I was overwhelmed with messages from listeners who had also been moved to tears and wanted to tell us what this moment had meant to them. They wanted to tell Jonny what an inspiration he was and how, even in the depths of their own sadness, they could now look at how he had clung on just that

'Having faith in yourself is
just a hugely radical act'

– JESSIE BURTON, AUTHOR

little bit longer when things seemed so inexpressibly bleak. A passing stranger had helped him. He had connected. And that moment of human connection had showed him something that made living worthwhile. That single act of kindness, that crucial glimpse of fellow feeling, had saved his life.

And so it's true to say, I think, that the expression of one's vulnerability is the ultimate show of strength. Being brave enough to share your wounds is an act of compassion that makes others feel less alone. In doing so, failure is reclaimed so that it no longer isolates but connects. This is a beautiful thing.

And if, like Jonny, you feel in the darkest despair, I implore you to just cling on.

Cling on for that little bit longer.

You never know what is going to happen next.

The real failure might be not finding out.

Yes, but do the Failure Principles actually work?

Short answer? Yes, because I'm not preaching a theoretical position. I have put these principles into practice myself. I know they work because of the story that follows.

Shortly after I came up with the idea for this book, I found out I was pregnant. Miraculously, unexpectedly so.

Throughout my thirties, I had tried and failed to have children. During the course of one particularly bleak year, I had two back-to-back cycles of IVF – with both, I got to the final stage of having an embryo re-implanted (the second time, it was two) and both times, the pregnancies failed to stick. A few months later, a naturally occurring pregnancy ended in a miscarriage at 12 weeks. By the end of 2014, I had technically been pregnant three times. I was flailing around in a sea of hormones, numbed by the shock of what my body had been through and struggling to process emotionally what I now realise was a form of slow-motion grief.

I miscarried in October and turned 36 in November. That Christmas, I faced the inescapable conclusion that my marriage had broken down. We rowed horribly on Christmas Eve.

'The worst loneliness is the one you feel in a couple,' said a friend I confided in at the time. He was right.

I kept trying to make it better, to make myself feel less isolated and more connected, as if the sheer force of my will would salve the wound. But slowly, I realised that one person could not make the relationship between two people work. It had to be both of us making the effort. That was the whole point. A marriage is a dialogue, not a monologue delivered repeatedly to a reluctant audience.

In February, I walked out of the home I shared with my husband. It was one of the hardest things I have ever done and also the only thing I could have done without erasing myself entirely. When, 18 months later, the divorce came through, there was no metaphorical cymbal-clash. A piece of typed paper headed 'Decree Absolute' seemed a curiously muted way to mark the complete transformation of self. But there it was, in black and white: the emancipation of myself from any pre-conceived ideas I had of the perfect woman I should be, replaced by the messy, liberating reality of the human I truly was. It took me a long time to stop pretending to be someone, to stop attempting to please everyone else while shrinking my own desires to an invisible point on some faraway horizon. After my marriage ended, I finally understood that you can't live in a cage constructed for you by the judgement or perception of others.

Nor can you trust your own expectations. I had always believed I would be a mother, but as I dated into my late thirties, any hope I had of having a biological child dwindled into a sliver of vanishing possibility. When, at 39, I met my partner, he already had three children. We had conversations about trying for a family, but we both felt that it was healthier to let fate take its course. We would see what happened. I didn't hold out much hope.

Sure enough, nothing did happen for a while.

But then, two weeks after my forty-first birthday: the unthinkable. My period was late. Not massively so, but enough for me to notice. I'd just had an extremely busy work patch involving a lot of travel and we'd moved house in the middle of it, so the conditions were – it must be said – sub-optimal for pregnancy. I was pretty sure that my period was late simply because it had been a stressful time.

Still, I was due to go out for dinner on one particular Friday, and I thought I'd take a pregnancy test just to reassure myself it would be safe to drink. I thought so little of it that I bought one at a pharmacy in a tube station – it was one of those places where the pharmacist serves you, so I didn't have a chance to check the test she'd given me. It turned out to be an old-fashioned one that showed two pink lines when you were expecting.

I stuffed the test in my handbag, then went for lunch at a nearby cafe. Afterwards, in the toilets downstairs, I took the test. I placed it on a tiled ledge as I washed my hands, and one strong pink line appeared. Well, I thought, that's it. I guess I'm not pregnant. It was disappointing but unsurprising. And besides, it meant I'd be able to have a glass of wine that evening.

But then, a fainter pink line appeared, as if a figure were walking towards me through fog. I discounted it at first. No, I thought, that's just where the moisture has gathered … it's too far away to mean anything else. The second line kept getting deeper in colour. But it seemed quite far away from the first one, as if it could simply be … I don't know … residue or something. I took out my phone to Google 'What does it mean when the lines on a pregnancy test are far apart?'

Google was fairly unanimous: it means you're pregnant.

Still, I left the restaurant unconvinced. So I bought another test – my own choice this time – and it was an expensive digital one that promised 99 per cent accuracy. I waited until I got home to take it and when the screen flashed up with 'Pregnant', I burst into simultaneous tears and laughter.

Later, when I told my partner, he also cried. It seemed such a magnificent, serendipitous thing: as though it shouldn't have happened and yet the universe had decided it would. It seemed as if it were somehow *meant to be*.

Being naturally pregnant for the second time was a curious mixture of deep, happy calm and a near-constant surface-level anxiety. Every time I went to the loo, I checked for blood. Every time my stomach gurgled, I felt panicked that this presaged the beginning of the end.

I rejoiced in my sore boobs and the feeling of tiredness, and I tumbled into uncertainty when the symptoms seemed briefly to disappear. I looked up everything on the internet. Why didn't I have cravings? What did it mean if my nose was dry? What yoga poses was I allowed to do? Why wasn't I getting morning sickness? Was I imagining the whole thing? And so on and so on.

I clung on for almost six and a half weeks, at which stage we went for an early scan with a lugubrious consultant who seemed to be running late for something.

'I like your tie,' I said, scrabbling to elicit some connection or fellow feeling, however superficial. It was one of those knitted, 1950s-style square ties with a geometric pattern in mustard yellows and muted greens.

He looked embarrassed.

'Thank you. They're made by a small British company.'

He didn't elaborate. I lay back on the chair, propping my legs up on the brackets and shuffling forwards as the nurse re-arranged the towel. The consultant inserted the ultrasound probe into my vagina and then tilted the screen towards me so that I could see what was happening. A semi-circle of murkiness appeared. And then: a fuzzy white patch. I was pregnant after all. I hadn't been imagining it. I breathed out.

The initial signs were good: there was a pregnancy, high up in the uterus, but he couldn't get a clear look at what was going on within the gestational sac. He fiddled around with the probe, while I winced with discomfort.

'This is a very small pregnancy,' he said. 'I can't see an embryo.'

I started to cry, the tears leaking out and falling on the paper lining placed over the tilted-back chair. I gripped my partner's hand tightly, and he returned the squeeze with equal force. Afterwards, we hugged in the street.

We went to a cafe for some tea and cake, and we discussed what it might mean. The consultant had not seemed positive, warning us that the chances of miscarriage were high, but I was still pregnant, wasn't I? Perhaps I had conceived later in my cycle than we thought, which would mean the pregnancy was not as advanced as we might have imagined? Perhaps it was all going to be fine. It had to be, I thought. The universe had decided this pregnancy was *meant to be*.

I took to the internet again. The advantage of online fertility forums is also their fatal flaw: you can find anything you want to be told. If there's a story that doesn't fit in with your own hoped-for narrative, you can discount it until you scroll through to the case study that offers you the most positive outcome. So I ignored the women who had undergone similar scans at six weeks, only to miscarry naturally in the ensuing days. I concentrated instead on all the women who said that seemingly empty gestational sacs turned into full-blown healthy pregnancies at the next scan – it was simply that measuring pregnancies was an imprecise science. Many of these women would sign off with something like 'And now my five-year-old daughter is sitting next to me as I type.'

I went to bed relieved. It was just a matter of timing.

The next day I started spotting. It was Friday 13th.

Again, the internet forums told me that was to be expected after a transvaginal scan. Again, I muted the ones that cautioned me to expect something else.

I miscarried on the day I was due to turn seven weeks pregnant, the blood coming slowly at first but then with irrefutable persistence. It was different from my first miscarriage, which had required a hospital stay. That time, the bleeding and the pain had been stemmed by an operation to remove what is called, with bleak clinical precision, 'early pregnancy remains'.

Now, I was advised to stay at home and bleed it out. It was barbaric. I was told by male doctors to expect something akin to 'a heavy period'. But it was much, much worse than that and I began to question where that comparison had come from.

The world of fertility medicine in Britain is still overwhelmingly dominated by men, and however gifted a male consultant might be, they have no first-hand experience of what a heavy period feels like, let alone a miscarriage. The effect of such language is to diminish a woman's pain. It is to imply that she mustn't make too much fuss and that an 'early' miscarriage is not something to bother a hospital with or something you would waste valuable medical resources on. It is to be endured behind closed doors, even if that means you end up lying on the floor, as I did, clutching your stomach in pain with each jagged surge of cramping, a towel underneath your body in case you stain the carpet with your blood.

I bled for days. I carried on with life as much as I could, but it was so odd taking part in normal interactions while losing our baby.

I was sad for a bit. Very sad. The kind of sad that doesn't shift; that lies beyond your own internal landscape like an incoming blizzard that turns the sky glowering grey.

I had failed at something I'd wished for beyond measure, and I had failed not because of a misjudgement or a mistake, but because of a pre-destined quirk of biology that could not have been anticipated or altered. It was the *pech* kind of failure and it was a direct challenge to put into practice the formula I had devised over the preceding months. Here it was: a failure that I needed to process and live with. Would the seven failure principles work?

Spoiler alert: they did.

They worked primarily because they helped me to realise that this failure was something happening to me rather than swallowing me up whole. I could see, for the first time, that the failure existed separately to who I was as a person, and this gave me a strange sense of calm. I knew there was hope, that if I gave it time, the pain would either pass or become livable with.

This wasn't an empty premise. I knew that this was a chance for me truly to understand whether the principles

THE SEVEN FAILURE PRINCIPLES

I had been telling other people to live by actually worked when I applied them to my own situation. I was critical. I attacked each one of them, half expecting them to let me down as if I could not quite allow myself to believe in the truth of what I'd devised.

It was, I now realise, the two parts of my psyche battling for supremacy. In the red corner, there was this embedded sense of never feeling that anything I said could have validity. This sprang from the imposter syndrome that many women are socially conditioned to feel; the idea that we should be grateful to have space on this earth and that we should, ideally, stay in our lanes and not cause too much trouble for the important people who are out there running things. I had this secret, power-ful, shameful fear that the failure principles wouldn't work and that I'd spent all this time preaching an unintentional falsehood to other people.

In the blue corner, I had a new way of being, seven principles to guide me, a philosophy – or a failosophy – forged through adversity; not only my own, but other people's, which was asking me to take charge of how I wanted to live my life, to make different decisions, to step into the possibility that the answers sprang from within, if only I could feel confident enough in my own instincts to trust in their guidance.

The blue won out. But it's important for me to state that, at first, it didn't seem to me to be a sure thing, and that it's only through genuine personal application that I can tell you these principles do actually work. At least, they did for me. They continue to do so.

There was a point, in the weeks after my miscarriage, when the sadness was still skulking around my ankles like an un-fed cat, that I voice-noted my friend Clare. I told her that part of what I found so difficult in accepting what had happened was the fact that I had believed the pregnancy was meant to be, and that I also firmly adhered to the view that things happened for a reason. That, as Max Ehrmann wrote in his 1927 prose poem, 'Desiderata': 'whether or not it is clear to you, no doubt the universe is unfolding as it should'. (I didn't quote this poem in the voice-note, because I am not *that* pretentious.)

'I'm struggling,' I said to Clare. 'If everything happens for a reason, what was the reason for this? It isn't clear to me.'

I had so fervently believed that this pregnancy would happen, I said, and my intuition – that gut feeling which exists separately from logical thought and which I have spent a lifetime trying to tune into – seemed to suggest it was so. How could I ever trust my instincts again?

Clare replied with the following:

'Sometimes, I feel like things are going to be OK and then they're not and then I question,' she said. 'But then I came to the conclusion that it is because you have peace that passes understanding. And sometimes we interpret that peace as "Things will work out the way that we think they'll work out" but actually, what it perhaps means is that you had an innate sense of peace within yourself no matter what, that can't be shaken. That doesn't mean that you have lost your intuition about who you are – more it means you've come to a deeper understanding of it. That's what I think it means. It means, I think, that you've come to a point in your life where all the things you've put into practice about being the truest you are working. And that doesn't negate the pain, but it does mean that you are a living, walking, breathing example of somebody who is courageous and who is doing the hard work.'

I've transcribed that voice-note word for word. This is actually how Clare speaks. She's basically a guru.

This, for me, was one of the biggest things I learned from the whole experience: that we can fail, and still be at peace. That we can believe things will work out for the best while also coming to terms with the fact that our understanding of the world is imperfect and that, whatever happens, if we work enough on our strength, our resilience and our acceptance of failure, we will be all right. More than all right, in fact. We will be fully realised people who understand that life is neither wholly good nor wholly bad, but a miraculous collage of myriad different experiences which we can strive to meet equally with grace. They will all teach us something worth knowing.

Conclusion

or What Does Failure Teach
You About Success?

'Things that might otherwise be perceived
as failures, I very often choose to
perceive as something else: as interesting,
or useful'

— MALCOLM GLADWELL, AUTHOR

I developed the seven Failure Principles as part of a live
How To Fail tour that began in early 2019. The tour
comprised 10 dates, in theatres around the UK (and one
in Dublin). The format was loosely the same in each city:
I came on stage at the beginning to outline each of the
principles and I would then introduce a special guest and
conduct an interview following the same format as the
podcast, with three of their failures providing the central

structure. Afterwards, there was an audience question and answer session.

When I first agreed to the tour, I was extremely nervous. I was uncertain that anyone would want to buy tickets, and anxious about agreeing to big venues before we had secured the guests. I was worried that no one would have questions they wanted to ask, and basically that the whole thing would turn out to be a giant stress nightmare brought to life: the one where I walked onto the centre of a vast and lonely stage, only to forget everything I wanted to say and be jeered at by the few audience members who were there.

This fear never entirely went away, even when the venues started to sell out. The most extraordinary thing for me to get my head around was that, as time went on, we were selling out before we had announced the special guest (quite often this was because we had failed to get one, but shhh, don't tell anyone that).

'What's happening?' I asked my tour manager, Serena.

'Well,' she said, looking at me with her customary unflappable calm, 'I think it's safe to say they're buying tickets to see *you*.'

In February 2020, we announced a one-off date at the National Theatre in London. The tickets sold out in 24 hours. It was at this point that I panicked. Selling out the National Theatre was something I had never once had the temerity to envisage for myself. It wasn't even the fulfilment of a dream – the dream itself would have seemed too far-fetched to allow myself to have in the first place. As a novelist, I was used to doing dispiriting book events at literary festivals, where I felt lucky to sell a couple of copies after a sparsely attended panel discussion in a draughty town hall where most people in attendance had come for the other, more successful writer I had been paired with.

Selling out the National Theatre was wonderful, but it was strange, too, because however much I tried, I could not silence that internal nagging voice that kept asking me 'Who on earth do you think you are? Get over yourself, love. What have you done to deserve this?'

It was not the first occasion on which I had experienced imposter syndrome – that ingrained feeling that you are a fraud who is about to be found out – but it was one of the most acute. I tried to analyse why this was. The conclusion I came to was that because the podcast had arisen out of an instinctive desire to do something which enabled us to be a little bit more vulnerable, that I weirdly felt the success of it didn't count. It had come so naturally to me that I hadn't once thought to strategise its future. If I hadn't planned this, and if I was just being myself out there, did I truly have enough right to claim the space? I had truly never anticipated it becoming a success and I certainly hadn't realised it would fundamentally change my life. The more the podcast grew, the more I grew with it and the more able I was to be the fullest expression of my authentic self in all aspects: professionally and personally.

To be rewarded for something that was already a reward in and of itself, felt greedy. And I think, at the root of this sensation, was the lie that we are taught about success.

We are taught to believe that success is external. We are taught to believe that success will come to us with job promotions, wealth, fame, designer clothes and superyachts. Success, we are told, is the ability to fly first class and accrue followers on Instagram and get tables at the hottest restaurants through the simple deployment of our name. We've been told that success is to be known by others, when in truth the most meaningful success is to know ourselves.

Of course, it doesn't serve the big corporations who want to sell us stuff to be content as we already are, imperfections and all. They want us to think that consumption is the key to happiness, and for that to work, we need to be kept in a state of constant unease.

On the night of the National Theatre show, as I waited in the wings for my cue to go on, I began to wonder. Could it possibly be true, I thought, as I took to the stage and looked out at the packed rows of seats in front of me, that being myself was enough to be worthy of *this*? And could I have been so bamboozled by the lies society tells us about success that I felt my most imposter-ish at precisely the moment I was being most fully myself? Could my worry that I was about to be found out simply be an old, default reaction scrabbling to make itself heard?

Because it's hard to re-wire your former ways of thinking, of being, if you've spent most of your life shaping the same neural pathways of self-doubt. The first few times you try to change the way you see the world and the first few times you attempt to look at failure as objective fact, not a negative verdict on who you are, your mind won't be used to it. It will kick back in opposition, wrongly believing that the familiar ways are the best. But just because something feels familiar does not mean it is good for you. Often, it means quite the opposite.

The music dimmed. The stage lights went up.

Yes, all this could be true.

Failure had helped me shed that skin of not-good-enough. Failure had stripped me back and built me up. It had broken me down and challenged me to grow. Failure, and learning how to deal with it, had made me more … well, *me*. The greatest realisation was that when I was most myself, people responded. They, in turn, felt more able to be honest with me. That creates an unassailable connection. That is the solidarity of failure.

Truman Capote wrote that 'failure is the condiment that gives success its flavour' and it's certainly true that life is a combination of light and shade, and that one cannot fully experience its highs unless we have also understood what it is to live through the lows. But I would go one step further and say that in choosing to learn from failure, we also redefine our expectations of success. Success for me now is about being able to be the fullest, most authentic expression of myself in all areas of my life and, in the process, forging stronger, more meaningful and more widespread connections with other human beings.

All of us can learn to fail better. It might seem strange or difficult or counterintuitive at first, but it gets easier with practice. With each failure that we choose to grow from, we become more ourselves. That, for me, is its own sort of success.

Failure continuously teaches us who we are.

It is nothing to be scared of.

Failure has been the making of me.

It might just be the making of you too.

Addendum:
A Catalogue of
Failure

In advance of recording a podcast season, I ask each of my guests to come up with three failures they don't mind discussing that will form the basis of the interview. I give them a completely free rein and tell them that the failures can be as profound or as lighthearted as they like.

I often think you can tell just as much about a person from the *type* of failures they choose as you can from the way they talk about them. People choose to list them in different ways – brief summations of a few words, in some cases; beautifully expressed miniature essays in others. Below is a short selection of examples.

David Baddiel, comedian, playwright and author

1. The moment a corporate gig in front of a lot of bankers went very wrong and led to me giving up stand-up for 10 years. It involves big swearing, this story. Hope that's OK.
2. My last adult novel, *The Death of Eli Gold*. I don't actually consider this a failure, in that I think it's my best novel. But that's kind of the point; it did fail, insofar as how success in literary fiction can be measured, and led to me giving it up, and writing children's books instead (commercially very successfully). So I thought it might be interesting to talk about.
3. My failure to score a penalty in a charity game at Villa Park, for a Comic Relief team.

Frankie Bridge, pop star

1. Failure to talk about mental health.
2. Failure to have a solo career.
3. Failure to live in the moment.

ADDENDUM: A CATALOGUE OF FAILURE

Alastair Campbell, writer, charity campaigner and former director of communications for Prime Minister Tony Blair

1. If you want one from childhood, I got beaten up in a fight when I was about seven or eight and I can remember telling myself I have to learn to stand up for myself: and learn to be OK with being on my own.
2. I guess my breakdown in 1986.
3. Not understanding sufficiently how much my job and my moods were impacting on [my partner] Fiona and the kids.

Fearne Cotton, broadcaster, podcaster and author

1. The first is one I didn't recognise as a failure at all at the time but had a lot of social expectation around it so I think it's an important one to discuss as many young people out there will be wracked with shame and also anxiety around it: I failed most of my GCSEs.

   I got As in Art, English and PE as I was naturally good at those, but the others I barely passed or failed or didn't even turn up to. I think I got six in the end.

I was already working at the time as I started in TV at 15 so I was away filming for two of them. I didn't see it as failure as I didn't feel I fitted into the academic curriculum at all, but I think the pressure on kids today is insane. I can see it even with my six-year-old. It's madness and we need to promote soft skills – making eye contact, being polite and working as a team – as valuable concepts in school too.

2. My second one again is based more on social pressure. At 29, I had a failed engagement. At that point I thought I'd know where I was headed personally and I was desperate to have kids. I don't want to talk about my ex-partner too much as I massively respect him and his new lovely wife but I think, again, there are a lot of pressures around marriage and knowing where you're headed as you hit 30, so I'm happy to talk about that and what I have learned.

3. My last one is more nebulous to some extent but leads me into new territory I feel I am now ready to discuss. My third failure is the failure to be myself for most of my twenties. In my teens I was vividly ME, then in my twenties I started to feel like I didn't fit in, like I wasn't enough and that I was somehow massively flawed. This mostly manifested in an eating disorder for nearly a decade. I had very bad bulimia in my early twenties and that then turned into an

on-off bad habit towards the latter half of the decade. It started because I felt like I didn't look right to be in the business I was in. I wasn't cool enough or smart enough or funny enough to be defined in the industry, so I felt very discombobulated. I have not talked about this at all, but I think it is time and your podcast feels like a nice and safe place to have this chat without making it some huge over-the-top deal. It's my last layer to peel back, I guess. It is now also why I am so dedicated to my health and how I eat and look after myself. I'm obsessed with food and cooking because I didn't allow myself the pleasure for so long. Only in the last few years have I started being ME 100 per cent again and it feels bloody good.

Ncuti Gatwa, actor

1. Not clearing my throat at my first singing audition: When I was about seven or eight my primary school had auditions for the school choir; I auditioned and got accepted with flying colours. I really loved singing, but secretly, so getting the chance to do so I was properly chuffed. I then got asked with a couple of other kids to audition for a citywide youth choir. My mum took the day off, we got the bus all the way out to the sticks, saw all the other kids from all the

other schools and I got a huge lump in my throat. I was so consumed by fear I was actually too afraid to cough or clear my throat before it was my turn to sing because God, for some reason I thought I'd get in trouble. I sang. Sounded like a frog. Didn't get into the choir.

2. Waking up late for my show at the Globe: I was playing two big roles at the Globe at the same time. Demetrius in *A Midsummer Night's Dream* and Adolphus in *946: The Amazing Story of Adolphus Tips*. Both directed by Emma Rice. Both amazing productions. I was going through a particularly tricky time in my personal life and I became particularly partial to going out on the lash as a form of letting stress go. At this particular height in my theatre career this started to become detrimental, and one night I got so hammered that I actually didn't wake up in time for my show the next day. The show started at one. I woke up at 12.57. It was not a good day.

3. Not developing more of a relationship with my dad: It works, the one we have, and I guess we're both happy, however I definitely could have been more receptive to his attempts to be a close figure in my life in the past, and also attempt to reach out a little more now.

Malcolm Gladwell, author

1. as a child i was a very successful age-class runner. i quit at 16, when it became clear to me that i was never going to be an Olympic-calibre athlete, and didn't take up serious running again until i was 50. i robbed myself of 35 years of doing something i love more than almost anything because i failed to understand how much pleasure there is in simple mediocrity.

2. once, in an article for the *new yorker* magazine, i quoted a passage from a book by the author charles murray, to the effect that murray believed that it made sense to segregate low-IQ people, to prevent them from reproducing. in fact, he meant the exact opposite. (i left out a crucial 'not'.) i made that mistake because i can't stand murray, and my disdain for him led me to imagine that he was capable of believing something ludicrously and implausibly monstrous. that shook me.

3. i had a very close friend who i realized, after many years of knowing her, was an alcoholic. a serious one. since i made that realization, our friendship has faltered. i realize i gave up on her. why and how that happened remains one of the most difficult questions i've ever dealt with.

[Gladwell wrote his email to me without any capital letters. When I asked him about this on the podcast, he replied, 'I didn't even know people used capital letters in emails any more. I haven't used them in 10 years. I kind of like the way it looks and … I don't know … I thought we all did this now?']

Dame Kelly Holmes, Olympic gold medallist

1. Failed at school.
2. Failed at first selection to be a Physical Training Instructor in the army.
3. Winning silver at the World Championships in 1995 because of nerves.

Cush Jumbo, actor

1. Failure to be perfect: I come from a big family, I'm one of six. Our family was unconventional to say the least. My dad was a very strict Nigerian who chose to stay at home and raise us while my mum went to work. My mum is from Scunthorpe and worked every hour she could to support us all. They met in their late teens and were both on the run from their pasts. They thought they could escape the past by

building a future of their own. To them that meant having six children. To us that meant being brought up by two people who had a lot of love to give but not a clue how to parent or 'adult'. I was the second oldest and so, along with my big sister, 'deputy' of the family. I was told from a young age that my job was to be responsible, to lead, to set the perfect example for the others, at school, at home and in life. So I developed a fear of letting my family down, of not making them proud, of being a disappointment, and I've carried that fear my whole life, it's affected every decision I've made. Recently, with the help of therapy and a wonderful husband and son, I've finally been able to start to kill this fear that has haunted me for years, but I still look over my shoulder for it constantly. It's a work in progress.

2. Failure to launch: I wasn't one of those actors who left drama school and shot into the stratosphere. I was the complete opposite. I left drama school at 20 with a first-class degree and no job in sight. I had an agent who didn't understand or believe in me and nothing to fall back on economically. I knew that I was good enough and talented enough and had something special to give but there are SO many other variables to being an actor than if you're good enough, and that's the most fucked-up thing about this business. On top of this lack of control and constant rejection I was incredibly economically

unstable. I had nothing but a bank account in the negative. Sometimes I didn't know what I'd eat at the weekend. I lost count of the number of times I'd beg a landlord to let me off the rent until the following month. My parents helped when they could, but they barely had anything themselves and I felt guilty every time I asked for help. Living hand to mouth can be exciting for some in their early twenties, but as you proceed you begin to see friends finding solid places to live, solid people to be with and purpose and success in their careers, and the more you see this the more you begin to feel as if the whole thing, life itself, is hopeless and that there is no point to your existence at all. I had never wanted to be anything else but an actor, but I was being told that that wasn't possible and that I was a failure. On top of that there was no safe place to hide or recover from it all, I was just too poor and around this time I went through the most horrible break-up, so I'd pretty much failed on all fronts. I moved home to my parents' house and dropped into a black hole of suicidal thoughts. After one particular day of obsessing about suicide so much that I knew I was beginning to plan it, I got up, put my shoes on, made an appointment at the doctor and told them that I didn't feel safe. A month later I'd got a dog (best thing I ever did!) and written the first draft of *Josephine and I* but only because I had to: it was write my way out or give up on life. I like to speak with young acting students about this stuff as much as I can so that they begin to understand how important caring for their mental health is in this job (they don't talk about it at drama school!) and how important it is to keep feeding yourself with joy and art when things aren't going your way creatively: with friends and family and galleries and plays and books and music and life.

3. Failure to have it all: So now we jump to years later. I've been so lucky and privileged. I have a wonderful husband and a flourishing career and then … I had a baby. Max is the most amazing thing, the most wonderful being, but his entry into my life has been my biggest challenge. Now I have to parent when my parents were never sure how and I need to do that on top of wife-ing and job-ing and woman-ing, and it's a lot. I'd been so focused on my career that I hadn't thought about children, in fact I didn't think I wanted them at all – I'd brought up enough bloody siblings – but it happened and it was a blessing and yet it was completely overwhelming. I hated being pregnant, but I didn't feel like I was allowed to admit it. I felt trapped and claustrophobic, but I couldn't say that. I worked 14-hour days through the whole pregnancy and never wanted to show any weakness in a business that doesn't view weakness or fuss well. I went back to work when my son was four months old and so I had to get back into shape almost as

soon as I'd had him. It was horrible and yet nobody told me that I had to, I just knew that I did. I struggle with the balance of my life every day. For a while I tried to do everything, perfectly, all the time and I've made this discovery that it's bloody impossible, it's a lie! It's a fallacy we (women) have been taught and a mantra we've been brainwashed with. But one day someone told me something really helpful – 'everything costs something', and once I'd made peace with that, life really started to make sense and I was much happier.

Tom Kerridge, chef

1. Education – GCSEs.
2. Failure at business (opened a bar at Clayton's in Marlow about nine or ten years ago, didn't succeed).
3. Failure at drinking … or just being very good at drinking …! Which has led to the issue of failing to live in the moment.

Marian Keyes, author

1. Failure to get into journalism college: I didn't learn anything, except to feel shame, and to feel that ambition was a painful thing to have. Reinforced my

belief that I was good at nothing, and that it would be better if I just made my peace with that. It kept me stuck in a job I was overqualified for. (In retrospect I would have been a terrible journalist. I just wanted to work with words. Maybe I was spared – I would have crashed and burned at some stage.)

2. Failure to have children: I love the idea of family, and that's why I keep writing about it. We talked of having six children, all with Irish names. To me, a proper family has millions of people in it.

   I learned that nobody gets everything, that we're in control of almost nothing. And even when you don't get what you want, it can still be delivered to you in other ways – in this case, nieces and nephews!

3. Putting on and losing the same two stone all my life: This teaches me many things – how insidious and prevalent fat phobia is, and how women's appearance is treated as a public commodity – the way that it's considered acceptable to criticise a woman's size, and to openly congratulate women when they make themselves smaller. I haven't found any resolution. It's a painful thing to live with – I know it's irrational, and one of the strands of sexism, but I wish I was thinner.

Jamie Laing, entrepreneur and reality TV star

1. Eight years old, parents got divorced, went to boarding school, my nanny of eight years left and we moved to London with my mum all in one go.
2. Eighteen years old, playing rugby on tour in Italy and I dislocated and snapped my ACL ligament and couldn't play rugby again (I'd had a blueprint of me becoming a rugby player all through my teens).
3. Thirty years old and haven't been able to cement a strong romantic relationship.

Karl Lokko, poet and former gang leader

1. Failing friends/community by initially believing the lie of the streets.
2. A failed music career? Really feeling that I let down all around me.
3. Not getting up the Matterhorn.

Mabel, pop star

1. Failure to sleep.
2. Failure to stay vegan.
3. Failure to remember lyrics.

Vicky McClure, actor

1. My work ... the number of failed jobs, auditions is countless.
2. School: I had a great time but failed miserably at the education side.
3. I've failed at a good few relationships mainly because I just did what they wanted ... young and stupid innit!!
4. One thing I can fail at daily is being spontaneous: if it's not arranged, organised, I can fail to enjoy whatever it is ... that pisses me right off. I'm a list-maker ... it can be a hindrance.
5. I fail at keeping up with exercise ... every single time I try!!!

Anyway, there's a few to keep you going – I'm sure over our chat a few more will spring to mind!! What a fucking failure!!

Ella Mills aka Deliciously Ella, businesswoman

1. Failure to embrace vulnerability – closing myself off when I was ill.
2. Failure to breastfeed.
3. Failure to accept failure – parts of our business so far.

Jess Phillips, politician

1. Failure in contraception [which resulted in the birth of her oldest son].
2. Failure to get onto Home Office fast track.
3. Failure to fix my brother's drug addiction.

Andrew Scott, actor

1. Failure at a drama competition for children, aged 10.
2. Failure at Trinity College Dublin as an academic.
3. Failure to be heteronormative.

Lemn Sissay, poet

1. I failed to marry. I failed to have children.
2. I failed to maintain the family I spent my life searching for.
3. I failed to become the poet I hope one day to be.

Nigel Slater, cook and author

1. I failed my father: My father was one of five children brought up by a single mum in Birmingham. He trained as a gunsmith, and later became an engineer. My father worked night and day building a large engineering company in the Black Country and assumed that his eldest son, my brother John, would take over the running of the business. He didn't want to. Neither did his second son, Adrian, who emigrated to Australia. I was my father's last hope of finding someone to inherit all his hard work. He was disappointed beyond words when I told him I wanted to cook instead. I think it broke his heart. He ended up selling the business for less than it was worth. I don't think he ever forgave me.

   I was a surprise to my parents. My older brother is 17 years my senior. When my mother was expecting me, she developed acute asthma that eventually led to her death. He never said as much, but I am pretty sure my father blamed me for her death. If she hadn't given birth to me, he wouldn't have lost her.

2. I failed to be a chef: I always knew I wanted to cook. I never thought of doing anything else. Assuming this, I did cookery at school (a big deal in the 1960s) and went on to hotel school (where I flourished) and then out into the world to work in restaurants and hotels. From the moment I put on my chef's whites, I knew there was something wrong. I felt like a clown.

I embarked on a roving apprenticeship in the starred restaurants of the day, getting more and more depressed with every job. Eventually it dawned on me that the one thing I had wanted to do in life just wasn't working for me. I hated everything about being a chef. I ran away from the worst place, a highly respected restaurant in the north of England, to Cornwall where I ran a bed and breakfast and antique shop with my sister-in-law.

In the winter there was no work, so I moved to London, slept on a friend's floor, and found work in a cafe. It was there I met a magazine editor who asked me if I would test some contributors' recipes for her magazine. It was the start of a 30-year career as a food writer.

3. I fail my friends: I am a terrible friend. I forget birthdays and break promises and can be quite flaky

socially. I am sure my friends have lost count of the number of times I have failed to do something I promised to. If you asked them to describe me in three words, I guarantee the word that would come up most often would be 'selfish'.

Meera Syal, actor, comedian, playwright and author

1. Following the Gina Ford method with my second child: when I had my second (and very late) child, 13 years after my first one, I'd forgotten pretty much everything. The baby guru Gina Ford was all the rage in 2005, so I mistakenly thought, well I'll follow the Gina Ford plan: I mean, everyone else having babies seems to be doing it, it's structured and sensible and within six weeks I should have a calm baby sleeping at six-hour intervals and feeding when I allow it. What a load of bullshit – I spent the first six months of my son's life feeling a failure at every aspect of mothering and so regret not following my instincts. He's now 13. Gina Ford taught me a valuable early lesson. You know your child, you know what they need. And if you don't, ask them, your partner, your mum or someone you trust with kids the same age. Don't get it out of a trendy bloody book. Written by a woman WHO HAS NEVER HAD CHILDREN.

2. Auditions – I'm terrible at them, I know that now: out of 20 I may possibly get one job – and only because usually I'm not that bothered about that particular job. I still get cold sweats remembering my one and only audition with one of my all-time heroines, Victoria Wood. It meant so much that I did possibly the worst audition of my life – I could see the hope trickling out her face, replaced by disappointment, then confusion, then boredom.

   I'm learning finally that walking into a room reeking of desperation is guaranteed to make you perform badly and for them to not want you. (I also learned this when I started producing and became the person on the other side of the table auditioning actors.) I've learned you need to walk in open, full of joy for the job you love and thinking, do I want to work with you, and can we work together and do something fantastic? And if you don't get the job, not to take it personally – hard when you're an actor and you're the product, as it were, but sometimes it's just not the right fit for a myriad of different reasons. That's meant to be someone else's gig and yours will be coming, if you're open to it.

3. Maths. Can't do it. Don't understand it. Obvs I can do basic tables, adding, subtraction, at a push 'bus stop' long division, but the minute it comes to algebra I'm done. I failed my Maths exam every single year I was in senior school, and I was a grafter.

Immigrant work ethic: if you aren't good at something, simply work harder and success will be yours. That never happened with Maths, possibly because I had a racist sadist for a teacher for years – the more I studied, the less intelligible it became. It's a nightmare being faced with something you can't fix no matter what you do. In desperation, because in those days you couldn't even apply to any uni without Maths O-level, in my O-level year my parents hired a Maths tutor. A loose term – he was one of their friends who yes, was a Maths graduate back in India, but in the UK he was an ice-cream man. He'd turn up to tutor me in his van, with the jingles on. Even now when I hear 'The Teddy Bears' Picnic' I break out into a cold sweat. Miraculously he got me through it. Somehow I scraped a C. After all that angst, sweat, money and tears, I scraped a C. This was the point where my parents realised I was never going to be a doctor, or anything vaguely scientific and they gave me their blessing to go on and study English and Drama: the only Asian girl anyone had ever heard of in our circles allowed to study such 'useless' subjects. The rest, I suppose, is history!

Lisa Taddeo, author

1. After my parents (in fact my whole family – dog included) died in my twenties, I stopped writing for a long time and used whatever money had come from selling our family home to buy myself expensive dinners, duck leg confit, foie gras, caviar, etc. I transferred from New York University (with full scholarship and truly fantastic class offerings, like a Virginia Woolf class of only 10 students) to Rutgers – a state school – for a boy. Then I smoked marijuana every day and lived with a young woman who used to dump her cat litter out into the bathtub (which was odd, since cat litter is meant to absorb liquid); then again, it was better than the suicidal roommate I'd lived with at NYU named Jenny, who ate her cereal out of a dog bowl and made Q-tip castles from used Q-tips.

2. Career-wise there were thousands of mini-failures, but I didn't allow them to stay failed. Not because I am tremendous or ambitious but because I am a Capricorn with OCD. When the editor of *Esquire* told me the first draft of the first story I ever wrote for them (MY BIG CHANCE) was good but not enough for print, only for online, I cried and smoked 50 cigarettes and then rewrote it until it was new and perfect that very night and sent it in the

next morning and they printed it. But it was a failure at first because I was trying to write what I thought THEY wanted and not what I wanted.

BONUS, BIGGEST ONE:

3. But truly, the biggest one is ongoing and I don't know when it will stop. I have miserable anxiety and coddle it daily. There are things to do with my daughter that I worry will happen again. And the terrible truth is that I never want to change. I suppose that is my most gigantic failure. I worry about death and my loved ones dying because, see number one. And I can't stop trying to control those things, or I can't work. Can't think.

Tracey Thorn, musician and author

1. Failing to get into the University of East Anglia – had a disastrous interview and they didn't offer me a place – I went to Hull instead, where I met Ben.
2. Failing my driving test – I took it again, and passed, but I was a terrible driver and always thought the fail was the correct result – I ended up crashing, and never drove again.

3. Failed to cure my stage fright with hypnotherapy – but it made me realise I was trying to get a quick fix for something that was a bigger issue, and I ended up going for proper therapy.

Phoebe Waller-Bridge, writer, actor and creator of *Fleabag*

1. Not realising what an impact *Fleabag* would have on my family.
2. Being a people-pleaser and not wanting to kick up a fuss.
3. Not tidying my room.